Series / Number 07-035

INTRODUCTION TO SURVEY SAMPLING

GRAHAM KALTON
University of Michigan

SAGE Publications
International Educational and Professional Publisher
Newbury Park   London   New Delhi

For information address:

SAGE Publications, Inc.
2455 Teller Road
Newbury Park, California 91320
E-mail: order@sagepub.com

SAGE Publications Ltd.
6 Bonhill Street
London EC2A 4PU
United Kingdom

SAGE Publications India Pvt. Ltd.
M-32 Market
Greater Kailash I
New Delhi 110 048 India

Printed in the United States of America

International Standard Book Number 0-8039-2126-8

Library of Congress Catalog Card No. 83-050475

98   99   00   01   02   21   20   19   18   17

When citing a university paper, please use the proper form. Remember to cite the Sage University Paper series title and include the paper number. One of the following formats can be adapted (depending on the style manual used):

(1) Iversen, G. R., & Norpoth, H. (1976). *Analysis of variance* (Sage University Paper series on Quantitative Applications in the Social Sciences, No. 07-001). Beverly Hills, CA: Sage.

OR

(2) Iversen, G. R., & Norpoth, H. 1976. *Analysis of variance*. Sage University Paper series on Quantitative Applications in the Social Sciences, series no. 07-001. Beverly Hills, CA: Sage.

CONTENTS

Series Editor's Introduction

Survey research is now a major enterprise both in the academic world and beyond. It is a basic tool in every social science and related discipline and is the foundation for such major research enterprises as the National Election Studies, the National Opinion Research Center's General Social Survey, and the Michigan Survey Research Center's extensive consumer surveys. It is frequently used in applied settings of all sorts, both for descriptive purposes and as a base for evaluation efforts. Last but certainly not least, it has achieved extraordinary visibility because of its use in political campaigns.

The foundation of survey research, of course, lies in sampling procedures. No matter how good the questions asked and no matter how elegant the analysis, little knowledge will be gained if the sample itself is poorly designed and executed. Despite the obviousness of these statements, one might think that sampling is simply a technical matter best left to statisticians. My view is quite different. While sampling statisticians are crucial to many projects, researchers directing and using surveys for substantive purposes should have at least a reasonable grasp of sampling principles. That is why we are so happy to add Graham Kalton's *Introduction to Survey Sampling* to our series.

Kalton's book takes a fine middle road toward explaining sampling procedures. It is not designed with the sampling statistician in mind. Rather, it is a highly readable text that will be understandable to those with a reasonable grasp of elementary statistics. All of the concepts are carefully illustrated, providing readers with a firm understanding of the major components of survey design. An important feature of the book is that it includes coverage of practical considerations. Sections on sampling frames and nonresponse, for example, could be ignored were it not for the problems one encounters in practice.

The fine coverage both of sampling theory and numerous practical problems make Kalton's book a valuable text for the beginning reader as well as for those who have previously learned some sampling theory.

—*Richard G. Niemi*
Series Co-Editor

INTRODUCTION TO
SURVEY SAMPLING

GRAHAM KALTON
University of Michigan

1. INTRODUCTION

Sample surveys are nowadays widely accepted as a means of providing statistical data on an extensive range of subjects for both research and administrative purposes. Numerous surveys have been conducted to develop, test, and refine research hypotheses in such disciplines as sociology, social psychology, demography, political science, economics, education, and public health. Central governments make considerable use of surveys to inform them of the conditions of their populations in terms of employment and unemployment, income and expenditure, housing conditions, education, nutrition, health, travel patterns, and many other subjects. They also conduct surveys of organizations such as manufacturers, retail outlets, farms, schools, and hospitals. Local governments equally make use of surveys for local planning purposes. Market researchers carry out surveys to identify markets for products, to discover how the products are used and how they perform in practice, and to determine consumer reactions. Opinion polls keep track of the popularity of political leaders and their parties and measure public opinion on a variety of topical issues.

In view of the currrent widespread use of surveys, it is somewhat surprising that the sample survey as we know it today has only a short history. This history is largely confined to the present century, and much of the growth in the use of surveys has occurred since the 1930s. During

AUTHOR'S NOTE: *I would like to thank Dick Niemi, Keith Rust, Tom Smith and Doug Zahn for their advice and suggestions on a draft version of this paper. Special thanks go to my wife, Francis, for her help in preparing the manuscript.*

this century considerable advances have been made in all aspects of survey methodology, and in particular in sampling methods, which are the subject of this paper. At the beginning of the century statisticians were debating whether anything less than a complete enumeration of a population would suffice, given that this was feasible in principle (O'Muircheartaigh and Wong, 1981). Since that time sampling has become widely accepted, and an impressive array of sampling methods has been devised to enable efficient and economic samples to be drawn in a variety of practical settings.

The design of a survey involves many interrelated decisions on such factors as the mode of data collection (whether by face-to-face interview, telephone interview, or self-completion form), the framing of the questions to be asked, and the method of processing the data, as well as the sample design (see, for instance, Moser and Kalton, 1971; Warwick and Lininger, 1975). Although this paper is concerned only with sample design, it needs to be recognized that in practice the sample design must be developed as an integral part of the overall survey design. In particular, the economics involved in the data collection process exert a considerable influence on the choice of sample design.

One of the first steps in survey design is to define the population to be studied. Here the term "population" is used in the technical sense of the totality of the elements under study, where the "elements" are the units of analysis. The elements may be persons, but they could alternatively be households, farms, schools, or any other unit. The population definition needs to be precisely and carefully specified according to the survey objectives, because the results will depend on the definition adopted. Consider, for instance, a survey to be carried out in a city to discover the degree of support for the introduction of a new bus system. Should the survey be confined to persons living within the city boundaries? What is the minimum age for the population to be surveyed? Should residents ineligible to vote in city elections be included? Should visitors living temporarily in the city be excluded, and if so, how are they to be defined? A variety of questions like these arise in defining most populations, making the definitional task less straightforward than it might at first appear.

It is a useful exercise to start by defining the population as the ideal one required to meet the survey objectives—the *target population*. This definition is then often modified to the *survey population* to take account of practical constraints. For instance, many national surveys in the United States would ideally include servicemen based abroad, people living in

Hawaii and Alaska, and people living in hospitals, hotels, prisons, army barracks, and other institutions. However, the severe problems involved in collecting responses from such persons frequently lead to their exclusion from the survey population. The advantage of starting with the ideal target population is that the exclusions are explicitly identified, thus enabling the magnitude and consequences of the restrictions to be assessed.

Once the population has been defined, the question of taking a sample from it can be addressed. One possibility, of course, is to take a complete enumeration of all the elements in the population, but this is seldom appropriate. To collect data from only a part of the population is clearly less costly and, providing the estimates are sufficiently precise, sampling is thus more economic. A sample inquiry can also be conducted and processed more speedily, leading to more timely reporting. Furthermore, by concentrating resources on only a part of the population, the quality of the data collection may be superior to that of a complete enumeration. As a result, a sample survey may in fact produce more accurate results. For these reasons, unless the population is small, sampling is almost always used.

The subject of sample design is concerned with how to select the part of the population to be included in the survey. A basic distinction to be made is whether the sample is selected by a probability mechanism or not. With a probability sample, each element has a known, nonzero chance of being included in the sample. Consequently, selection biases are avoided, and statistical theory can be used to derive properties of the survey estimators. Nonprobability sampling covers a variety of procedures, including the use of volunteers and the purposive choice of elements for the sample on the grounds that they are "representative" of the population. The weakness of all nonprobability sampling is its subjectivity, which precludes the development of a theoretical framework for it. A sample of volunteers or a representative sample chosen by an expert can be assessed only by subjective evaluation, not by assumption-free statistical methods. In view of this weakness, this paper is restricted to probability sampling. Some discussion of nonprobability sampling is, however, included in Chapter 13.

An essential requirement for any form of probability sample is the existence of a *sampling frame* from which the sampled elements can be selected. In a simple case, when a list of all the population elements is available, the frame may be the list. When there is no list, the frame is some equivalent procedure for identifying the population elements.

Area sampling provides a good illustration of such a frame. With this technique, each element of the population is associated with a particular geographical area (e.g., people or households are associated with the area of their residence, or main residence if they have more than one). Then a sample of areas is drawn, and either all elements in the selected areas are included in the survey or a sample of these elements is included (see Chapter 12). The general organization of the sampling frame and the information it contains about the population elements often have a strong influence on the choice of sample design. Defects in the frame, such as a failure to cover all the elements in the survey population, can have harmful effects on the sample. Sampling frames are discussed in more detail in Chapter 8.

A variety of probability sampling techniques have been developed to provide efficient practical sample designs. Among the most widely used are systematic sampling, stratification, multistage (cluster) sampling, and probability proportional to size sampling. The following sections discuss these techniques separately for ease of exposition, but in practice they are employed together in what often become complex designs. Two examples are given in Chapter 12 to illustrate how the techniques may be combined. We begin with relatively simple techniques suitable for sampling small, compact populations and later turn to the more complex techniques needed for sampling larger, more widespread populations.

2. SIMPLE RANDOM SAMPLING

Simple random sampling (SRS) provides a natural starting point for a discussion of probability sampling methods, not because it is widely used—it is not—but because it is the simplest method and it underlies many of the more complex methods. As a prelude to defining simple random sampling, we will introduce the notation that the sample size is given by n and the population size by N. Then, formally defined, simple random sampling is a sampling scheme with the property that any of the possible subsets of n distinct elements from the population of N elements is equally likely to be the chosen sample. This definition implies that every element in the population has the same probability of being selected for the sample, but the definition is more stringent than this. As we will see later, more complex sampling methods are also often equal probability selection methods (epsem), but with such designs the joint probabilities of sets of elements being selected are not equal, as they are with SRS.

We will discuss simple random sampling in terms of a specific application. Suppose that a survey is to be conducted in a high school to find out about the students' leisure habits. A list of the school's 1872 students is available, with the list being ordered by the students' identification numbers. These numbers range from 0001 to 1917, with a few gaps in the sequence occurring because some students allocated numbers have since left the school. Suppose that an SRS of n = 250 is required for the survey. (The choice of n is discussed in Chapter 11.)

One way to draw the required SRS would be by a lottery method. Each student's name or identification number is put on one of a set of 1872 identical discs. The discs are placed in an urn, they are thoroughly mixed, and then 250 of them are selected haphazardly. If these operations were perfectly executed, the selected discs would identify an SRS of 250 students. Although conceptually simple, this method is cumbersome to execute and it depends on the assumption that the discs have been thoroughly mixed; consequently, it is seldom used.

Another way of selecting the SRS is by means of a table of random numbers. These tables are carefully constructed and tested to ensure that in the long run each digit, each pair of digits, and so on, appears with the same frequency. An extract from a table of random numbers produced by Kendall and Smith (1939) is given in Table 1.

Since the student identification numbers contain four digits, we need to select the random numbers in sets of four. In practice, one should start at some casually chosen point in the table, but here for simplicity we will start at the top left-hand corner. We will then proceed down the first set of four columns, down the second set of four columns, and so on. Numbers outside the range of the student numbers (0001-1917), and numbers within range but not associated with a current student, are ignored. The first four numbers in the table (6728, 8586, 4010, 9455) do not yield selections, so the first student selected is 1163 (provided this student is still at the school). Continuing through the table, the only other selections from this part of the table are 0588 and 0385. It is already clear that the selection of 250 students in this way is a tedious task, requiring a large selection of random numbers, most of which are nonproductive.

The waste of so many random numbers can be avoided by associating each student with several random numbers instead of just one; provided

TABLE 1
Random Sampling Numbers

67	28	96	25	68	36	24	72	03	85	49	24
85	86	94	78	32	59	51	82	86	43	73	84
40	10	60	09	05	88	78	44	63	13	58	25
94	55	89	48	90	80	77	80	26	89	87	44
11	63	77	77	23	20	33	62	62	19	29	03

SOURCE: Kendall, M. G. and B. B. Smith, *Tables of Random Sampling Numbers*. Copyright © 1939 by Cambridge University Press. Reprinted by permission.

that all the students are associated with the same number of random numbers, the sample remains an SRS. Here each student could be associated with five four-digit random numbers. A simple scheme is for student 0001 to be associated also with 2001, 4001, 6001, and 8001; student 0002 also with 2002, 4002, 6002, 8002; and so on through student 1917, who is associated also with 3917, 5917, 7917, and 9917. Then, again starting at the top left-hand corner of the table, the selected students are 6728 = student 0728; 8586 = student 0586; 4010 = student 0010; 9455 = student 1455; 1163 = student 1163, and so on.

In drawing the sample using a table of random numbers it is possible for an element to be selected more than once. This possibility does not exist with the lottery method described above, because when an element's disc was drawn from the urn it was not replaced to be given a further chance of selection. It would, however, also exist with the lottery method if at each draw the selected disc were replaced in the urn before the next selection was made. If sampling is carried out without replacement, the sample must contain n distinct elements, but with sampling with replacement the sample of size n may contain less than n distinct elements. When the sampling procedures described here are conducted with replacement, the sampling method is known as *unrestricted random sampling* or simple random sampling with replacement. When they are conducted without replacement, the method is known as simple random sampling without replacement or just *simple random sampling*. The selection of a simple random sample without replacement from a table of random numbers involves simply ignoring repeat selections of an element already in the sample. Since sampling without replacement gives more precise estimators than sampling with replacement we will concentrate on the without replacement method.

Having selected the SRS of 250 students, we will now assume that the data have been collected and that we have responses from all those sampled (issues of nonresponse are taken up in Chapter 9). The next step is to summarize the individual responses in various ways to provide estimates of characteristics of interest for the population, for instance, the average number of hours of television viewing per day and the proportion of students currently reading a novel. At this point we need to introduce some notation. Following a common convention in the survey sampling literature, capital letters are used for population values and parameters, and lower-case letters for sample values and estimators. Thus $Y_1, Y_2, \ldots Y_N$ denote the values of the variable y (e.g., hours of television viewing) for the N elements in the population, and $y_1, y_2, \ldots y_n$ are the values for the n sampled elements; in general the value of variable y for the ith element in the population is Y_i $(i = 1, 2, \ldots N)$, and that for the ith element in the sample is y_i $(i = 1, 2, \ldots n)$. The population mean is given by

$$\bar{Y} = \sum_{i=1}^{N} Y_i/N$$

and the sample mean by

$$\bar{y} = \sum_{i=1}^{n} y_i/n$$

In survey sampling the element variance of the y variable in the population is generally defined as

$$S^2 = \sum_{i=1}^{N} (Y_i - \bar{Y})^2/(N - 1)$$

and the sample element variance as

$$s^2 = \sum_{i=1}^{n} (y_i - \bar{y})^2/(n - 1)$$

Sometimes, however, the population element variance is defined with a denominator of N rather than (N—1), in which case it is denoted by

$$\sigma^2 = \sum_{i=1}^{N} (Y_i - \bar{Y})^2/N$$

(i.e., $\sigma^2 = (N - 1)S^2/N$).

Suppose that we wish to use the data collected in the survey to estimate the mean number of hours of television viewing per day for all students in the school, $\bar{Y}$. This raises the question of how good the sample mean $\bar{y}$ is as an estimator of $\bar{Y}$. With $\bar{Y}$ being unknown, this question is unanswerable for a specific estimate from a particular sample; instead, reliance has to be placed on the properties of the estimator on average over repeated applications of the sampling method. Observe here that the term *estimate* is used for a specific value, while *estimator* is used for the rule of procedure used for obtaining the estimate. In the present example an estimate of 2.20 hours of television viewing may be computed by substituting the values obtained from the sampled students in the estimator $\bar{y} = \Sigma y_i / n$. Statistical theory provides a means of evaluating estimators but not estimates. The following paragraphs briefly review the theory of statistical inference in the context of SRS; for a more complete discussion of statistical inference the reader is referred to a statistics text, e.g., Blalock (1972).

The properties of sample estimators are derived theoretically by considering the pattern of results that would be generated by repeating the sampling procedure an infinite number of times. In the present example, suppose that the operations of drawing an SRS of 250 students from the 1872 students and then calculating the sample mean for each sample were carried out an infinite number of times (of course, replacing each sample in the population before drawing the next sample). The resulting set of sample means would have a distribution, known as the *sampling distribution* of the mean. Provided that the sample size is not too small—often an n of 10 or 20 is sufficient—statistical theory shows that this distribution approximates the *normal distribution*, and that the mean of this distribution is the population mean, $\bar{Y}$. If the mean of the individual sample estimates over an infinite number of samples of the given design equals the population parameter being estimated, then the estimator is said to be an *unbiased* estimator of that parameter. Thus, in the case of an SRS, $\bar{y}$ is an unbiased estimator of $\bar{Y}$.

Although the sampling distribution of $\bar{y}$ is centered on $\bar{Y}$, any one estimate will differ from $\bar{Y}$; hence, a measure of the variability of the individual estimates around $\bar{Y}$ is needed. A common measure of variability is the standard deviation, the square root of the variance. In this case, the required standard deviation is that of the sample means in the sampling distribution. To avoid confusion with the standard deviation of the element values, standard deviations of sampling distributions are known as *standard errors*. We denote the sample mean of an SRS by $\bar{y}_0$ (with the subscript 0 to indicate simple random sampling), its standard error by $SE(\bar{y}_0)$ and the square of the standard error, the variance of $\bar{y}_0$, by $V(\bar{y}_0)$. For convenience, most sampling error formulae will be presented in terms of variances rather than standard errors. The variance of a sample mean of an SRS of size n is given by

$$V(\bar{y}_0) = \frac{N-n}{N-1} \frac{\sigma^2}{n} \qquad [1]$$

or equivalently by

$$V(\bar{y}_0) = \left(\frac{N-n}{N}\right) \frac{S^2}{n} = (1-f) \frac{S^2}{n} \qquad [2]$$

where $f = n/N$ is the sampling fraction.

These formulae show that $V(\bar{y}_0)$ depends on three factors: first, $(N-n)/(N-1)$ or $(1-f)$, either of which is called the finite population correction (fpc)—there is a negligible difference between these terms when N is large; second, n, the sample size; and third S^2 or σ^2, the alternative versions of the element variance of the y values in the population. The fpc term reflects the fact that the survey population is finite in size, unlike the infinite populations assumed in standard statistical theory, and that sampling is conducted without replacement. With an infinite population or if sampling were conducted with replacement, there would be no fpc term, in which case formula 1 would reduce to the familiar form $V(\bar{y}_0) = \sigma^2/n$. The fpc term indicates the gains of sampling without replacement over sampling with replacement. For samples of size 2 or greater, the fpc term is less than 1, which demonstrates that $\bar{y}$ calculated from an SRS is more precise—that is, has a smaller variance —than $\bar{y}$ calculated from an unrestricted sample of the same size. In many practical situations the populations are large and, even though the samples may also be large, the sampling fractions are small. In this situation the difference between sampling with and without replacement is unimportant because, even if the sample is drawn with replacement, the chance of selecting an element more than once is slight. This argument can also be expressed in terms of the fpc term. If the sampling fraction (f) is say $1/10$, the fpc term is 0.9 and its effect on the standard

14

error is as a multiplier $\sqrt{1-f} = 0.95$; if $f = 1/20$, $(1-f) = 0.95$ and $\sqrt{1-f} = 0.97$. These results show that if the sampling fraction is small, the fpc term is close to 1 and has a negligible effect on the standard error. The fpc term is commonly neglected (i.e., treated as 1) when the sampling fraction is less than 1 in 20, or even 1 in 10.

The second factor in the formulae for $V(\bar{y}_0)$ is the sample size, n. As is intuitively obvious, the larger the sample, the smaller is $V(\bar{y}_0)$. What is perhaps less obvious is the fact that for large populations it is the sample size rather than the sampling fraction that is dominant in determining the precision of survey results. For this reason, a sample of size 2000 drawn from a country with a population of 200 million yields about as precise results as a sample of the same size drawn from a small city of 40,000 (assuming the element variances in the two populations are the same). It also follows from this line of argument that the gains from sampling are greatest with large populations. Indeed, for very small populations, the gains from sampling may not be worthwhile, even though the fpc term has an appreciable effect in such cases. It may, for example, turn out on balance to be more convenient to take all students in a school of 200, rather than sample 175 of them.

The third factor in the formulae for $V(\bar{y}_0)$ is the element variance of the y-values in the population, either σ^2 or S^2. Clearly, if all the students watch approximately the same amount of television, the mean of any sample will be close to the population mean. However, if they differ greatly in their viewing habits, there is a risk that the sample mean will differ considerably from the population mean. Note that σ^2 and S^2 are population parameters; hence, they are unknown quantities in a practical application. In order to estimate $V(\bar{y}_0)$, an estimate of the population element variance is needed. The advantage of using formula 2 for $V(\bar{y}_0)$, expressed in terms of S^2, is that the familiar sample estimator $s^2 = \Sigma(y_i - \bar{y})^2/(n-1)$ is an unbiased estimator for S^2 (but not for σ^2). Thus $V(\bar{y}_0)$ and $SE(\bar{y}_0)$ may be simply estimated by

$$v(\bar{y}_0) = (1 - f)\, s^2/n \qquad [3]$$

and

$$se(\bar{y}_0) = \sqrt{(1 - f)\, s^2/n} \qquad [4]$$

with lower case letters for $v(\bar{y}_0)$ and $se(\bar{y}_0)$ to indicate sample estimators.

Having estimated the standard error, a confidence interval can be calculated for the population mean. For instance, with a large sample, the 95% confidence interval for $\bar{Y}$ is $\bar{y}_0 \pm 1.96$ se($\bar{y}_0$), where the 1.96 is taken from a table of the normal distribution (95% of the normal distribution falls within 1.96 standard deviations around the distribution's mean). As an illustration, suppose that the mean hours watching television per day for the 250 sampled students is $\bar{y}_0 = 2.192$ hours, with an element variance of $s^2 = 1.008$. Then a 95% confidence interval for $\bar{Y}$ is

$$2.192 \pm 1.96 \sqrt{\left(1 - \frac{250}{1872}\right)\frac{1.008}{250}} = 2.192 \pm 0.116$$

That is, we are 95% confident that the interval from 2.076 to 2.308 contains the population mean.

In addition to the mean, another parameter of common interest is the proportion (or percentage) of the population with a particular attribute, for instance the proportion of students currently reading a novel. Results for a proportion follow directly from those for a mean, since a proportion is just a special case of a mean. This may be seen by setting $Y_i = 1$ if the ith element has the attribute and $Y_i = 0$ if not. Then $\bar{Y} = \Sigma Y_i / N$ is simply P, the population proportion with the attribute, and the sample mean $\bar{y}$ is the sample proportion p. Thus, in general, theoretical results obtained for a sample mean apply also for a proportion. In the present case of simple random sampling, since $\bar{y}_0$ is unbiased for $\bar{Y}$, it follows that p_0 is unbiased for P. The standard error and variance formulae given above for $\bar{y}_0$ can also be applied to p_0. However, since the y variable takes values of only 0 or 1, the formulae for S^2 and s^2 can be simplified in the case of a proportion to $NPQ(N - 1)$ and $np_0q_0/(n-1)$, respectively, where $Q = 1 - P$ and $q_0 = 1 - p_0$. Using these simplifications,

$$V(p_0) = (1 - f)\frac{NPQ}{(N - 1)n} \qquad [5]$$

and

$$v(p_0) = (1 - f)\frac{p_0q_0}{(n - 1)} \qquad [6]$$

If the fpc term can be neglected, and if n is large, $v(p_0)$ reduces to the popular form p_0q_0/n. These formulae also apply with percentages, with the modification that $Q = 100 - P$ and $q_0 = 100 - p_0$.

As an illustration, suppose that 165 of the 250 sampled students were reading a novel, i.e., $p_0 = 66.0\%$. A 95% confidence interval for P is then

$$66.0 \pm 1.96 \sqrt{\left(1 - \frac{250}{1872}\right) \frac{66 \times 34}{249}} = 66.0 \pm 5.5\%$$

i.e., we are 95% confident that the interval 60.5% to 71.5% contains the population percentage.

The preceding discussion reviews the steps involved in estimating a population mean or proportion from an SRS and calculating an associated confidence interval. The general approach is the standard one for statistical inference from large samples, and the only distinctive feature is the inclusion here of the fpc term. The approach can also be used for the estimation of other population parameters.

3. SYSTEMATIC SAMPLING

Although the use of a table of random numbers to select the simple random sample of 250 students as discussed in the previous section was manageable, the operation was nevertheless somewhat laborious. Moreover, it would have been more laborious had the population been larger, the sample been larger, or the list of students not been ordered by identification numbers. The widely used method of systematic sampling provides a means of substantially reducing the effort required for sample selection. Systematic sampling is easy to apply, involving simply taking every k^{th} element after a random start.

As a simple example, suppose that a sample of 250 students is required from a school with 2000 students. The sampling fraction is 250/2000, or 1 in 8. A systematic sample of the required size would then be obtained by taking a random number between 1 and 8 to determine the first student in the sample, and taking every eighth student thereafter. If the random number were 5, the selected students would be the fifth, thirteenth, twenty-first, and so on, on the list.

The application of systematic sampling to the example in the last section is slightly more complicated than above, because the sampling fraction is 250/1872 or 1 in 7.488: thus, in this case the sampling interval, 7.488, is not a simple integer. Sometimes this problem can be satisfactorily handled by rounding the interval to an integer, with a resultant change in the sample size. In this example a 1 in 7 sample would produce a sample of 267 or 268, while a 1 in 8 sample would produce a sample of 234. If the variation from the planned sample size caused by rounding is not acceptable, alternative solutions are available. One is to round the interval down (to 1 in 7), to start with a student selected at random from the 1872 students in the population, and to proceed until the desired sample size (250) has been achieved. With this procedure, the list is treated as circular, so that the last listing is followed by the first. A second solution is to use a fractional interval, rounding down each time to determine the selection. In the present example, the random start is chosen as a four-figure random number from 1000 to 7488—say, 3654. Inserting a decimal place after the first figure gives 3.654, so that the first selection is the third student. Adding 7.488 repeatedly to 3.654 gives 11.142, 18.630, 26.118, and so on. The subsequent selections are then the eleventh, eighteenth, twenty-sixth, etc., students. The interval between selected students is sometimes 7 and sometimes 8.

One way to identify the students selected for the systematic sample would be to count through the list to find out which ones are the third, eleventh, eighteenth, and so on, on the list. An alternative procedure takes advantage of the student identification numbers. With this procedure the sampling interval is continually added until the resulting total exceeds 1917, the highest identification number. The rounded down numbers determine the selected students as before; in cases in which there is no student with the selected number, no selection is made. The expected sample size remains at 250, but the achieved sample size may deviate from this figure because of chance fluctuations in the fraction of blank numbers sampled.

Like SRS, systematic sampling gives each element in the population the same chance of being selected for the sample; i.e., it is an epsem design. It differs, however, from SRS in that the probabilities of different sets of elements being included in the sample are not all equal. For instance, in the first example of a 1 in 8 sample, the probability that elements 1 and 2 are both in the sample is 0, while the probability that elements 1 and 9 are both in the sample is 1/8, since if element 1 is in the sample element 9 is bound to be as well. The epsem property of systematic sampling implies that the sample mean is a reasonable estimator of the population mean. However, the unequal probabilities of sets of elements means that the SRS standard error formulae are not directly applicable with systematic sampling.

With the 1 in 8 systematic sample, the sampling distribution of a mean or proportion is easily determined: Since there are only eight different possible samples, each of which is equally likely, the sampling distribution is the eight sample means or proportions, each with probability 1/8. A limitation of systematic sampling is that, unless some assumption is made about the ordering of the list, the variability among the values of the sampled elements does not provide a basis for estimating the variability of the sampling distribution. To demonstrate this point consider again the estimation of the percentage of students currently reading a novel. Suppose that 1500 of the 2000 students are doing so, and that the school list happens to be ordered in repeated cycles of six readers followed by two nonreaders. The samples associated with the random starts from 1 to 6 would then contain all readers (p = 100%) while those associated with the random starts 7 and 8 would contain no readers (p = 0%). The sample estimator is in fact extremely imprecise, with a true standard error of 43.3%. The internal variability within any one of the eight possible samples is, however, zero, and hence it provides no indication of the magnitude of the standard error.

In order to estimate the standard error of estimators based on systematic samples, some form of assumption about the population needs to be made. Sometimes it is reasonable to assume that the list is approximately randomly ordered with respect to the survey variables, in which case the sample can be treated as if it were a simple random sample; lists arranged in alphabetical order may often be reasonably treated in this way. Sometimes the list may be ordered in groups (e.g., students by grade), with variability expected between groups in the levels of the survey variables. In this case a systematic sample may be analyzed as if it were a stratified sample (see Chapter 4). Survey samplers often rearrange the order of a list before drawing a systematic sample so as to obtain the gains of proportionate stratification.

As illustrated above, systematic sampling performs badly when the list is ordered in cycles of values of the survey variables and when the sampling interval coincides with a multiple of the length of the cycle. If, however, the sampling interval is not a multiple of the length of the cycle, systematic sampling from a list ordered in cycles can fare well. This can be seen by considering the effect of a 1 in 7 sample in the above example of student readers. While sampling practitioners need to be alert to the potential dangers of systematic sampling when sampling from lists with cyclical arrangements, such lists are rarely met in practice, and situations in which they may occur are usually easily recognized. Systematic sampling is widely used in practice without excessive concern for the damaging effects of undetected cycles in the ordering of the list.

4. STRATIFICATION

A commonly encountered feature of survey sampling is that a certain amount of information is known about the elements of the population to be studied. In selecting an area sample of the United States, for instance, information is available on the geographical location of the area, whether it is an inner city, suburban or rural area, and census information will provide a wealth of other information about the area—for instance, its population at the previous census, its rate of population change, the proportion of its population employed in manufacturing, and the proportion of its population with race reported as "not white." Supplementary information of this type can be used either at the design stage to improve the sample design, or at the analysis stage to improve the sample estimators, or both. This section discusses the use of supplementary information to improve the sample design through the technique of stratification.

The essence of stratification is the classification of the population into subpopulations, or strata, based on some supplementary information, and then the selection of separate samples from each of the strata. The benefits of stratification derive from the fact that the sample sizes in the strata are controlled by the sampler, rather than being randomly determined by the sampling process. Often the strata sample sizes are made proportional to the strata population sizes; in other words, a *uniform sampling fraction* is used. This is known as *proportionate stratification*. The division of the total sample between the strata does not, however, have to be restricted to a proportionate allocation; *disproportionate stratification* is also possible. In this section we will consider only the use of simple random sampling within strata, but as will be seen later, other sampling methods can also be used.

The notation introduced earlier needs to be extended to cope with the separate strata; this is done by adding a subscript h to existing symbols to denote the corresponding quantities in stratum h. Thus N_h is the population size and n_h is the sample size in stratum h, with $N = \Sigma N_h$ and $n = \Sigma n_h$ being the total population and sample sizes; $f_h = n_h/N_h$ is the sampling fraction in stratum h; $\overline{Y}_h$ and $\overline{y}_h$ are the population mean and sample mean in stratum h; and S_h^2 and s_h^2 are the population element variance and sample element variance in stratum h. It is useful to add a new symbol $W_h = N_h/N$ for the proportion of the population in stratum h, with $\Sigma W_h = 1$.

Given simple random sampling within strata, the preceding results can be applied to each stratum separately to show that the $\overline{y}_h$'s are unbiased for the $\overline{Y}_h$'s and that their variances and standard errors may be estimated according to formulae 3 and 4. The new problems presented by stratified sampling are how to combine the strata sample means to produce an estimator of the overall population mean $\overline{Y}$ and how to estimate the variance of this estimator. The solution to the first problem is readily obtained by noting that $\overline{Y}$ can be expressed as $\Sigma N_h\overline{Y}_h/N = \Sigma W_h\overline{Y}_h$. Hence an obvious estimator of $\overline{Y}$ is produced by substituting the strata sample means $\overline{y}_h$'s for the unknown $\overline{Y}_h$'s. This unbiased estimator is (with subscript st for stratified) $\overline{y}_{st} = \Sigma W_h\overline{y}_h$.

Selecting the samples in the various strata separately and independently, the variance of $\overline{y}_{st} = \Sigma W_h\overline{y}_h$ is given by standard statistical theory as

$$V(\overline{y}_{st}) = \Sigma W_h^2\, V(\overline{y}_h) \tag{7}$$

With SRS within strata, this formula becomes

$$V(\overline{y}_{st}) = \Sigma W_h^2(1 - f_h)S_h^2/n_h \tag{8}$$

on substituting formula 2 for $V(\overline{y}_h)$. An estimator of $V(\overline{y}_{st})$ is then obtained by substituting s_h^2 for the unknown S_h^2 in formula 8:

$$v(\overline{y}_{st}) = \Sigma W_h^2(1 - f_h)s_h^2/n_h \tag{9}$$

Proportionate Stratification

The above formulae apply for any allocation of the sample across the strata. In the case of proportionate stratification, i.e., a uniform sampling fraction with $f_h = f$ or $n_h/N_h = n/N$, these formulae simplify.

Proportionate stratification is an epsem design in which $\bar{y}_{st}$ reduces to the simple sample mean

$$\sum_h \sum_i y_{hi}/n$$

where y_{hi} is the y-value for the ith sampled element in stratum h, and the summation is over all the sampled elements. The variance of $\bar{y}_{st}$ in equation 8 reduces in this case to

$$V(\bar{y}_{st}) = (1 - f)\sum W_h S_h^2/n = (1 - f)S_w^2/n \qquad [10]$$

where $S_w^2 = \sum W_h S_h^2$ is the weighted average within stratum variance. Then $V(\bar{y}_{st})$ may be estimated by

$$v(\bar{y}_{st}) = (1 - f)\sum W_h s_h^2/n \qquad [11]$$

It may be noted that the variance of the mean based on a proportionate stratified sample—formula 10—is similar to that of a mean based on a simple random sample—formula 2. The only difference is that the population element variance S^2 in the SRS formula is replaced by the weighted average within stratum variance S_w^2 in the proportionate stratified formula. As an approximation with large N_h it can be shown by a standard analysis of variance decomposition that

$$S^2 \doteq S_w^2 + \sum W_h(\overline{Y}_h - \overline{Y})^2$$

Since the last term in this formula is a nonnegative quantity (a sum of squared terms), it follows that $S^2 \geq S_w^2$; in other words, a proportionate stratified sample cannot be less precise than an SRS of the same size. For a given total variability in the population, the gain in precision arising from employing a proportionate stratified sample rather than an SRS is greater the more heterogeneous are the strata means or, equivalently, the more homogeneous are the element values within the strata.

As illustrated in the preceding discussion, simple random sampling serves as a useful benchmark against which to compare other sample designs. A commonly used measure for this comparison is the *design effect*, the ratio of the variance of the estimator based on the complex design to the variance of the estimator based on an SRS of the same size. We denote the design effect of any estimator z by $D^2(z) = V(z)/V(z_0)$.

The design effect for the mean of a proportionate stratified sample is thus $D^2(\bar{y}) = S_w^2/S^2$, a number no greater than 1 under the above approximation. For some purposes the ratio of standard errors rather than variances is a more appropriate measure; the square root of the design effect is denoted by $D(z)$. A sample estimate of a design effect for z is denoted by $d^2(z)$. An alternative definition of the design effect makes the comparison with unrestricted sampling rather than with simple random sampling. This alternative has the attraction of comparing the complex sample variance with that given in standard statistics texts. However, since the difference in variances between SRS and unrestricted sampling is only the fpc term $(1 - f)$, which can generally be neglected, the difference in definition is mostly of minor importance.

To illustrate the use of proportionate stratification we return to the high school example of the previous chapters. We now suppose that the list of students is divided into four separate lists, one for each grade level (ninth, tenth, eleventh, and twelfth). The grades constitute the strata from which separate samples are drawn. Columns 2 and 3 of Table 2 give the numbers and proportions of the high school population in each grade. Column 4 gives the sample sizes taken from each stratum under a proportionate allocation with a uniform sampling fraction of 250/1872 or 1 in 7.488. Columns 5, 6, and 7 give the sample totals, sample means, and sample element variances in each of the strata for the number of hours per day of television viewing. Columns 8 and 9 give the numbers and proportions of sampled students in each stratum currently reading a novel.

The overall sample mean of the number of hours per day of television viewing can be computed from the general stratified formula as $\Sigma W_h\bar{y}_h$, but since the sample is a proportionate one, it can equally be calculated as the simple sample mean

$$\bar{y}_{st} = \underset{h\ i}{\Sigma\Sigma}y_{hi}/n = 548/250 = 2.192$$

In the same way, the overall sample percentage of students reading novels can be calculated as $p_{st} = 100\Sigma r_h/n = 100(163/250) = 65.2\%$. The variance of $\bar{y}_{st}$ can be calculated from formula 11 to give

$$v(\bar{y}_{st}) = \left(1 - \frac{250}{1872}\right)\frac{0.8808}{250} = 0.003053$$

TABLE 2
Proportionate Stratified Sample of High School Students
(hypothetical data)

(1)	(2)	(3)	(4)	(5)	(6)	(7)	(8)	(9)
Stratum	N_h	W_h	n_h	$\sum_i y_{hi}$	$\bar{y}_h$	s_h^2	r_h	p_h
9th grade	524	0.28	70	168	2.40	0.941	35	50%
10th grade	487	0.26	65	169	2.60	1.088	39	60%
11th grade	449	0.24	60	123	2.05	0.804	45	75%
12th grade	412	0.22	55	88	1.60	0.643	44	80%
Total	1872	1.00	250	548			163	

and

$$se(\bar{y}_{st}) = 0.0553$$

Thus, a 95% confidence interval for $\overline{Y}$ is $\bar{y}_{st} \pm 1.96\ se(\bar{y}_{st})$, or 2.08 to 2.30.

The estimated variance of p_{st} can also be obtained from formula 11, noting from earlier that $s_h^2 = n_h p_h q_h/(n_h - 1)$ for a percentage. Then

$$v(p_{st}) = \left(1 - \frac{250}{1872}\right)\frac{2160}{250} = 7.486$$

and

$$se(p_{st}) = 2.736\%$$

A 95% confidence interval for P is then given by $p_{st} \pm 1.96\ se(p_{st})$ or 59.8% to 70.6%.

The design effects for $\bar{y}_{st}$ and p_{st} may be estimated by s_w^2/s^2. In the case of $\bar{y}_{st}$, s^2 is approximately 1.008 (calculations not shown; see Cochran, 1977: section 5A11), so that $d^2(\bar{y}_{st}) = 0.8808/1.008 = 0.87$. In other words, an SRS of $250/0.87 = 286$ is needed to give the same precision as this proportionate stratified sample of 250. This sizable gain in precision of the stratified design results from the marked variation in the mean number of hours of television viewing of the different grades.

In the case of p_{st}, s^2 is approximately 2278, so that $d^2(p_{st}) = 0.95$. The gains from stratification may appear smaller than expected, given the substantial differences in the four strata percentages given in column 9 of Table 2. The relatively small gain with percentages is, however, the rule, unless some strata with extremely high (say over 90%) or extremely low percentages (under 10%) can be formed.

Disproportionate Stratification

Proportionate stratification is much used because it produces simple estimators and because it guarantees that the estimators are no less precise than those obtained from a simple random sample of the same size. There are, however, situations in which a disproportionate allocation is helpful.

One purpose of disproportionate stratification is to achieve an allocation that maximizes the precision of the estimator of the population mean within the available resources. The optimum allocation for this purpose is to make the sampling fraction in a stratum proportional to the element standard deviation in that stratum and inversely proportional to the square root of the cost of including an element from that stratum in the sample, i.e., $f_h \propto S_h/\sqrt{c_h}$, where c_h is the cost per sample element in stratum h. As might be anticipated, this result indicates that more heterogeneous strata and strata where costs are lower should be sampled at higher rates. Often the costs do not differ between strata, so that the optimum allocation reduces to $f_h \propto S_h$, the so-called Neyman allocation.

A practical difficulty to the use of optimum allocation is lack of firm knowledge of the stratum element variances and costs on which the allocation is based. Fortunately, reasonably accurate estimates suffice, for the loss of precision associated with minor departures from the optimum allocation is small. Another difficulty arises from the multipurpose nature of surveys, for what is an optimum allocation for one estimator may be a poor one for another. Unlike the situation with proportionate stratification, a disproportionate allocation can produce less precise estimators than the same-sized simple random sample.

Another use of disproportionate stratification is to allocate a sufficient sample size to certain strata in order that separate estimates of adequate precision will be available for them. Sample estimates are often required not just for the total population, but also for various subpopulations, which are termed *domains of study*. When a small stratum represents a domain of study, it is likely that a proportionate allocation will generate too small a sample from the stratum to produce sufficiently precise estimators; the remedy is to sample from that stratum at a higher rate.

Yet another situation that gives rise to a disproportionate allocation is when the survey aims to make comparisons between the stratum estimates rather than to aggregate them into an overall estimate. For instance, the purpose of the high school survey might be to compare the amounts of television viewing of the different grade levels rather than to calculate an overall estimate. When there are only two strata, the optimum allocation for estimating the difference between the stratum means is

$$\frac{n_1}{n_2} = \frac{(S_1/\sqrt{c_1})}{(S_2/\sqrt{c_2})}$$

If, as is often a reasonable approximation, stratum variances and costs are equal, the optimum allocation reduces to $n_1 = n_2$. Notice that, for comparisons between strata, the stratum population sizes are irrelevant, but they are important in forming the overall estimate. When both comparisons and overall estimates are required, stratum sizes that differ greatly can cause a conflict for the sample allocation. For instance, if stratum variances and costs are equal and the first stratum comprises 90% of the population and the second 10%, the optimum allocation of a sample of 500 for estimating the overall mean is 450 in the first stratum and 50 in the second, whereas the optimum allocation for estimating the difference between the two stratum means is 250 in each stratum. When this situation arises, the optimum allocation for one purpose can be extremely damaging for the other, but sometimes a reasonable compromise solution can be found.

As an illustration of the analysis of a disproportionate sample, we return once more to the high school example. The data in Table 3 have been arranged to conform to those in Table 2, except for the modifications made to adjust for the revised, disproportionate allocation of the sample in column 4. The chosen allocation divides the sample of 250 as equally as possible between the four strata, as might be done if each stratum were also to be treated as a domain of study (assuming that the strata element variances and costs were equal).

The overall mean number of hours of television viewing is computed from the formula $\bar{y}_{st} = \Sigma W_h \bar{y}_h$ as 2.192, the same value as before. In this

TABLE 3
Disproportionate Stratified Sample of High School Students
(hypothetical data)

(1)	(2)	(3)	(4)	(5)	(6)	(7)
Stratum	N_h	W_h	n_h	$\sum_i y_{hi}$	$\bar{y}_h$	s_h^2
9th grade	524	0.28	63	151.2	2.40	0.941
10th grade	487	0.26	63	163.8	2.60	1.088
11th grade	449	0.24	62	127.1	2.05	0.804
12th grade	412	0.22	62	99.2	1.60	0.643
Total	1872	1.00	250			

case, the simple mean $\sum\sum y_{hi}/n = 2.165$ is not a valid estimate of $\bar{Y}$: The higher grades, which are overrepresented in the sample, report less television viewing, and as a result, the simple mean underestimates $\bar{Y}$. The weighted mean corrects for the imbalance in the sample by weighting by the population stratum proportions W_h. The variance of $\bar{y}_{st}$, estimated by formula 9, is $v(\bar{y}_{st}) = 0.003117$, so that $se(\bar{y}_{st}) = 0.0558$. Comparing this standard error with that obtained with the proportionate allocation (0.0553) shows that this disproportionate allocation produces a marginally less precise estimator of the overall population mean.

Choice of Strata

Two conditions need to be fulfilled for standard stratification: First, the population proportions in the strata, the W_h's, need to be known, and second, it has to be possible to draw separate samples from each stratum. Techniques for handling the situation in which stratification is desired but these conditions are not met are discussed later. (See Chapter 10 on poststratification and Chapter 7 on two-phase sampling.) Provided that these conditions are met, there is considerable flexibility in the ways in which the strata can be formed. The only other restriction is that there must be at least one selection sampled from each stratum; otherwise it would not be possible to calculate an unbiased estimator of the overall population mean. If the sample is also to provide a standard error estimate, there must be at least two selections per stratum.

In practice, there often exists a considerable amount of information about the population that can be used for stratification purposes, thus providing a good deal of room for choice in how the strata are formed. This choice is determined by the objectives for the stratification. For gains in precision of the overall estimates, the strata should be formed to be as internally homogeneous in terms of the survey variables as possible. If separate estimates are needed for small domains of study, each domain should be placed in a separate stratum—or a set of strata— which can then be sampled at a higher rate to produce the required sample size. Sometimes it is useful to form strata within which different sampling methods can be employed. In surveying the population of a small city and its neighboring rural area, for instance, it may be desirable to take a systematic sample of households in the urban stratum while using area sampling in the rural stratum.

We return to the high school example to illustrate the joint use of several stratification factors. We now assume that, in addition to grade level, the following variables are available for use in stratification: student's sex, an overall academic performance score (categorized into three classes—high, medium, and low), and area of residence (categorized into three areas). Each of these variables is believed to be related to the student's amount of television viewing; in the case of area of residence, the justification for this belief is that the areas differ in their types of housing, and area may therefore serve as a proxy for family social class. There is no need to apply objective rules in using these variables for forming strata. The strata may in fact be created in any subjective way without risk of bias in the survey estimators; the use of probability sampling within strata protects against selection bias. The measure of success achieved in forming strata is their internal homogeneity, which of course affects the standard errors of the survey estimators. In this example, sex may be thought to be an unimportant explanatory variable for television viewing among ninth- and tenth-grade students, but an important one among eleventh- and twelfth-grade students. On the other hand, it may turn out that nearly all the eleventh- and twelfth-grade students come from only one of the areas of residence, so this variable is not a distinguishing factor for the older students. Taking account of these points, we may then form the strata as follows: First stratify the students by grade level; then within the eleventh and twelfth grades separate the students into the three performance classes and subdivide them into boys and girls, and within the ninth and tenth grades, separate the students into the three performance classes and subdivide them by the three areas of residence. This procedure produces 30 strata. If some strata turn out to be too small (say less than 15 students, a number that warrants 2 selections for a sample of 250 from a proportionate design), they can be combined with adjacent strata.

A problem that arises from the formation of numerous strata with a proportionate design is that the sample sizes required from some strata may be small and fractional. For example, applying the required sampling fraction of 1 in 7.488 to a stratum containing only 19 high school students gives a required sample size of 2.54. While rounding large sample sizes to the nearest integer will have only a negligible effect on selection probabilities, this does not hold for such small numbers. A common way to avoid the problem of fractional sample sizes is to employ "implicit" rather than "explicit" stratification. Implicit stratification involves listing the population by strata, then taking a systematic sample throughout the list. By this means, the stratum of 19 students would have either 2 or 3 selections, depending on the random number chosen to start the procedure.

5. CLUSTER AND MULTISTAGE SAMPLING

In most sampling problems the population can be regarded as being composed of a set of groups of elements. One sampling use for such groups is to treat them as strata, as discussed in the previous section. In this case, separate samples are selected from each group. Another sampling use is to treat them as clusters, in which case only a sample of them is included in the survey. If all the elements in selected clusters are included in the sample, the method is known as *cluster sampling*. If only a sample of elements is taken from each selected cluster, the method is known as *two-stage sampling*. Often a hierarchy of clusters is used: First some large clusters are selected, next some smaller clusters are drawn within the selected large clusters, and so on until finally elements are selected within the final-stage clusters. Thus, for instance, a survey of students in a state might first select a sample of schools, then samples of homeroom classes within selected schools, and finally samples of students within selected classes. This general method is known as *multistage sampling*, although it is also sometimes loosely described as cluster sampling.

Although strata and clusters are both groupings of elements, they serve entirely different sampling purposes. Since strata are all represented in the sample, it is advantageous if they are internally homogeneous in the survey variables. On the other hand, with only a sample of clusters being sampled, the ones selected need to represent the ones unselected; this is best done when the clusters are as internally heterogeneous in the survey variables as possible. Proportionate stratification is used to achieve gains in precision. On the other hand, except in special circumstances, cluster sampling leads to a loss in precision compared with an SRS of the same size. The justification for cluster sampling is the economy it creates for sampling and data collection. Unless this economy permits a sufficient increase in sample size to more than offset the associated loss in precision, the use of cluster sampling is inappropriate.

In this section, for simplicity, we make the unrealistic assumption that all the clusters are of the same size, B. (The next section discusses unequal-sized clusters.) From the A clusters in the population, $\underline{a}$ are sampled by SRS, and all the elements in selected clusters are enumerated. (Note: Wherever the letter "a" is underlined in the text, it signifies that it is being used as a mathematical symbol, rather than an article.) The sample size is n = aB and the sampling fraction is f = n/N = aB/AB = a/A. In the population, let $Y_{\alpha\beta}$ denote element β in cluster α, let

$$\bar{Y}_\alpha = \sum_\beta^B Y_{\alpha\beta}/B$$

be the mean of cluster α, and let

$$\bar{Y} = \sum_\alpha^A \sum_\beta^B Y_{\alpha\beta}/N = \sum_\alpha^A \bar{Y}_\alpha/A$$

be the population mean. In the sample, the corresponding quantities are

$$\bar{y}_\alpha = \sum_\beta^B y_{\alpha\beta}/B$$

and

$$\bar{y}_c = \sum_\alpha^a \sum_\beta^B y_{\alpha\beta}/n = \sum_\alpha^a \bar{y}_\alpha/a$$

With equal-sized clusters, the population mean is the simple mean of the A cluster means and the sample mean is the simple mean of the $\underline{a}$ sampled cluster means. As a consequence, the SRS of clusters can be viewed as an SRS of $\underline{a}$ means from a population of A means. It therefore follows immediately that $\bar{y}_c$ is unbiased for $\bar{Y}$ and that its variance is given from formula 2 as

$$V(\bar{y}_c) = \left(1 - \frac{a}{A}\right) \frac{S_a^2}{a} \qquad [12]$$

where

$$S_a^2 = \sum_{\alpha}^{A} (\bar{Y}_\alpha - \bar{Y})^2/(A - 1)$$

is the variance of the cluster means. It also follows that

$$v(\bar{y}_c) = \left(1 - \frac{a}{A}\right) \frac{s_a^2}{a} \qquad [13]$$

is an unbiased estimator of $V(\bar{y}_c)$, where

$$s_a^2 = \sum_{\alpha}^{a} (\bar{y}_\alpha - \bar{y})^2/(a - 1)$$

Comparing $V(\bar{y}_c)$ with the variance of the mean from an SRS of size n = aB gives the design effect for $\bar{y}_c$ as

$$D^2(\bar{y}_c) = \frac{S_a^2/a}{S^2/aB} = \frac{BS_a^2}{S^2}$$

The magnitude of $D(\bar{y}_c)$ depends on the ratio of the sizes of S_a^2 and S^2, and this ratio depends on the way the clusters are formed. For instance, suppose that the number of clusters A in the population is large and that the clusters are formed at random, then S_a^2, being the variance of means of SRSs of B elements each, would be approximately S^2/B. Under these conditions, $D^2(\bar{y}_c) = 1$, as might otherwise be anticipated. If, as generally applies, the clusters are more internally homogeneous than would occur from a random allocation, the cluster means will be correspondingly more heterogeneous; hence S_a^2 will be larger than S^2/B, so that $D^2(\bar{y}_c)$ will be greater than 1.

An informative alternative expression for the design effect of a cluster sample mean is

$$D^2(\bar{y}_c) \doteq 1 + (B - 1)\rho \qquad [14]$$

where ρ is the intraclass correlation coefficient measuring the degree of cluster homogeneity (Kish, 1965: section 5.4). If in a large population the clusters are formed at random, $\rho \doteq 0$; hence $D^2(\bar{y}_c) = 1$, as already established. A negative value of ρ, indicating that the clusters are more internally heterogeneous than would occur if they were formed at random, is possible, but ρ cannot be less than $-1/(B - 1)$. A negative ρ produces a design effect of less than 1, indicating that cluster sampling is more precise than SRS in this case. In practice, however, negative ρ's occur extremely rarely. As a rule, ρ's are small positive values (mostly under 0.15), so that $D^2(\bar{y}_c) > 1$. The maximum possible value of ρ is 1, which occurs when within each cluster all the elements have the same value.

As an illustration, we return again to the high school example. We suppose now that at a particular hour the school comprises A = 78 classes each of B = 24 students, and that it is inexpensive and convenient to have all the students in selected classes fill in the survey's self-completion questionnaire at that hour. A sample of a =10 classes, producing a sample of 240 students, is selected. The following numbers represent the proportions of students reporting reading a novel in each of the ten classes:

$$\frac{9}{24}, \frac{11}{24}, \frac{13}{24}, \frac{15}{24}, \frac{16}{24}, \frac{17}{24}, \frac{18}{24}, \frac{20}{24}, \frac{20}{24}, \frac{21}{24}$$

The overall proportion is $p_c = 160/240 = 66.7\%$. From formula 13 the variance of this estimate, with $p_\alpha = \bar{y}_{\alpha'}$ and $p_c = \bar{y}_c$, is given by

$$v(p_c) = \left(1 - \frac{10}{78}\right) \frac{0.02816}{10} = 0.002455$$

so that se(p_c) = 0.04955 or 4.96%. Since s_a^2 is based on only 9 degrees of freedom, the t distribution rather than the normal distribution should be used in forming a confidence interval for the population percentage. Thus a 95% confidence interval for P is 66.7 ± 2.26(4.96) or 55.5% to 77.9%, where the figure 2.26 is the tabulated 95% point for the t distribution with 9 degrees of freedom.

The value of v(p_c) may be compared with the variance of the proportion based on an SRS of the same size. This variance is given from formula 6 by

$$v(p_0) = \left(1 - \frac{240}{1872}\right) \frac{0.6667 \times 0.3333}{239} = 0.0008106$$

so that se(p_0) = 0.02847 or 2.85%. The design effect for the cluster sample proportion is thus

$$d^2(p_c) = 0.002455/0.0008106 = 3.029$$

Using formula 14 an estimate of ρ is then given by

$$\hat{\rho} = [d^2(p_c) - 1]/(B - 1) = 0.088$$

These results show that the positive intraclass correlation has caused the cluster sample to be much less precise than an SRS of the same size. Approximately, ignoring the effect of the fpc term, the cluster sample needs to be three times as large as the SRS to give the same degree of precision.

As formula 14 makes clear, the design effect of a cluster sample mean depends on two factors, the intraclass correlation ρ and the cluster size B. The sizable design effect in the above example comes about because of a fair degree of homogeneity in the amount of television viewing within classes—or, equivalently, a fair degree of heterogeneity between classes—together with a class size of 24 students. Even if ρ is small, the design effect can be large if the multiplier (B – 1) is large. Had the class size been, say, only 8 with the same degree of homogeneity, the design effect would have been reduced to 1.62. In practice, the value of ρ generally tends to increase the smaller the cluster, but usually at a slow rate so that the reduction in B exerts the dominant effect on the design effect.

With cluster sampling this argument suggests that, providing the clusters are large enough to secure the required savings in costs of sampling and data collection, the smaller the size of the clusters the better. When, as often applies, there is a hierarchy of clusters, the smallest ones meeting the requirements will generally be the preferred choice. In the high school example, the students could be grouped by grade levels or classes; here grade levels are too large to serve as clusters for sampling purposes, and classes are the obvious choice. The problem with cluster sampling is that, because clusters usually comprise existing groupings that were formed for other purposes, the lowest level of clustering still often yields clusters that are too large to be used efficiently in cluster sampling. The obvious solution to this problem is to divide the clusters into subclusters for sampling purposes; essentially this is what is done in multistage sampling.

Consider a two-stage sample in which $\underline{a}$ clusters are selected by SRS from the A in the population, and then SRSs of b elements are taken from the B elements in each selected cluster. The simple sample mean

$$\bar{y}_{ts} = \overset{a}{\underset{\alpha}{\Sigma}}\overset{b}{\underset{\beta}{\Sigma}} y_{\alpha\beta}/n = \overset{a}{\underset{\alpha}{\Sigma}}\bar{y}_{\alpha}/a$$

is still an unbiased estimator of the population mean but note now that

$$\bar{y}_{\alpha} = \overset{b}{\underset{\beta}{\Sigma}} y_{\alpha\beta}/b$$

is the sample mean for cluster α, not the true mean for that cluster as it was with complete cluster sampling. The variance of $\bar{y}_{ts}$ is

$$V(\bar{y}_{ts}) = \left(1 - \frac{a}{A}\right)\frac{S_a^2}{a} + \left(1 - \frac{b}{B}\right)\frac{S_b^2}{ab}$$

where

$$S_b^2 = \overset{A}{\underset{\alpha}{\Sigma}}\overset{B}{\underset{\beta}{\Sigma}}(Y_{\alpha\beta} - \bar{Y}_{\alpha})^2/A(B-1)$$

is the average element variance within the clusters. The first term in this formula is that for cluster sampling, and the second term represents the additional variance accruing through the subsampling within selected clusters. If $b = B$, the second term is zero and the formula reduces to the variance of a cluster sample mean given by formula 12. If $a = A$, all the clusters are included in the sample; hence they are strata. The first term is zero when $a = A$, and the second term is the variance of the mean with a proportionate stratified design as in formula 10: $f = b/B$, $n = ab$, and $S_w^2 = S_b^2$.

An unbiased estimator of $V(\bar{y}_{ts})$ is given by

$$v(\bar{y}_{ts}) = \left(1 - \frac{a}{A}\right)\frac{s_a^2}{a} + \frac{a}{A}\left(1 - \frac{b}{B}\right)\frac{s_b^2}{ab}$$

where

$$s_a^2 = \sum_{\alpha}^{a}(\bar{y}_\alpha - \bar{y})^2/(a - 1)$$

and

$$s_b^2 = \sum_{\alpha}^{a}\sum_{\beta}^{b}(y_{\alpha\beta} - \bar{y}_\alpha)/a(b - 1)$$

This formula is somewhat laborious to compute because s_b^2 involves calculating the sample element variances in each of the selected clusters. If the first-stage sampling fraction a/A is small, the second term in $v(\bar{y}_{ts})$ is small; hence, as an approximation, it may be dropped. This leads to the estimator

$$v(\bar{y}_{ts}) = s_a^2/a \qquad [15]$$

which is simple to compute. In essence, the approximation treats the first-stage sampling as being carried out with, rather than without, replacement. Providing the first-stage sampling fraction is small, as it often is in practice, the approximation is adequate. The approximation is widely used with complex sample designs, and it is employed in most computer programs for sampling errors from such designs.

Another approximation to the two-stage design considers each cluster in the population as conceptually divided into B/b ultimate clusters (UCs) of b elements each. With the present design, in which subsampling is conducted by SRS, the UCs are viewed as being formed by SRS within each cluster. Within each cluster, first an SRS of b elements is taken to comprise the first UC, then an SRS of b elements is taken from the remaining elements to comprise the second UC, and so on until B/b UCs are formed and all the elements are accounted for (we assume here for simplicity that B/b is an integer so that the last UC is also of size b). Then an SRS of UCs is drawn from the population of AB/b UCs, with all the elements in the selected UCs being included in the sample. This sample design is a close approximation to the two-stage design discussed above. It differs in that the two-stage design selects only one UC from each sampled cluster, whereas this restriction does not apply with the ultimate cluster design. However, providing a/A is small, the chance of selecting two UCs from the same cluster with the ultimate cluster design is small; under this condition the ultimate cluster design serves as a satisfactory approximation to the two-stage design. The attraction of the ultimate cluster sample design approximation is its simplicity: It is a sample of complete (ultimate) clusters, and the formulae for cluster sampling can be immediately applied. Thus, for instance, an approximate variance estimate for $V(\bar{y}_{ts})$ comes directly from formula 12 as

$$v(\bar{y}_{ts}) = \left(1 - \frac{ab}{AB} \right) \frac{s_a^2}{a} \qquad [16]$$

where the sampling fraction is $a/(AB/b) = ab/AB = n/N$ and s_a^2 is the variance of the means of the sampled UCs. Under the condition of the approximation to the two-stage design (i.e., that a/A is small), the fpc term can be dropped, thus yielding the same variance estimator as the with-replacement approximation.

For the ultimate cluster sample design, the design effect for the sample mean is given from formula 14 as $1 + (b - 1)\rho$, where ρ is the intraclass correlation in the UCs and b is the size of the UCs. When the UCs are formed by SRS, their expected homogeneity is the same as that in the original clusters. Thus, as an approximation, the design effect for the two-stage sample is

$$D^2(\bar{y}_{ts}) \doteq 1 + (b - 1)\,\rho \qquad [17]$$

As formula 17 shows, if ρ is positive, the design effect declines as the subsample size b declines: for a fixed total sample size n = ab, the smaller the subsample size, and hence the larger the number of clusters included in the sample, the more precise is the sample mean. However, the more spread the sample is across clusters, the higher will be the survey costs, and hence the smaller the sample that can be obtained for a fixed budget. These two factors have to be balanced against each other to determine the optimum combination of the number of sampled clusters, $\underline{a}$, and the number of elements drawn from each selected cluster, b. For this purpose, a model of the survey's cost structure needs to be specified. A simple cost model is $C = aC_a + nc$, where C is the total cost, C_a is the cost per sampled cluster, and c is the cost per sampled element. Under this model, the optimum choice for b that minimizes the variance of the sample mean is approximately (Kish, 1965: section 8.3B)

$$b_{opt} \doteq \sqrt{\frac{C_a}{c} \; \frac{(1 - \rho)}{\rho}} \qquad [18]$$

It follows from this formula that, other things being equal, the sample should be more spread across clusters (i.e., a smaller value for b) the greater the cluster homogeneity, the greater the element cost, and the smaller the cluster cost. If, say, the relative cost C_a / c is estimated at 17 and $\rho = 0.07$, $b_{opt} = 15$. Given the total budget, the number of clusters to be sampled can then be determined.

The cost model used in the derivation of b_{opt} is an oversimplified one, but it is probably adequate for general guidance. More sophisticated models can be used, but it is doubtful whether the added complexity is worthwhile. The estimation of cost components proves to be extremely difficult even for the simple model. In addition to costs, the estimation of b_{opt} also requires an estimate of ρ. This estimate may often be based on past surveys involving similar variables and similar sample designs. Since surveys are multipurpose, with different variables having different values of ρ, the choice of b involves some degree of compromise between several different optima.

The use of multistage sampling is justified by economies achieved in sampling and data collection. The sampling economies are considerable with area sampling, where the lists from which elements are selected need be compiled only in the selected final-stage clusters (e.g., city blocks or smaller segments). With data collection by face-to-face interviewing, multistage sampling can give substantial savings in interviewer travel costs. If the population is a large, widely scattered one, a single-stage sample would be thinly spread, whereas a multistage sample concentrates the interviews in a number of locations. Clustering provides no significant data collection economies with telephone interviewing or mail questionnaires (unless face-to-face interviewing is used for follow-up inquiries or to deal with nonrespondents), but with telephone interviewing clustering can give sampling economies (see Chapter 12).

Suppose that a household survey is to be conducted by face-to-face interviewing in a particular city. If the city is small and a list of households (or dwellings) is available, a single-stage sample, probably stratified by area and other variables, may be the best choice. If the city is small but no list is available, a two-stage design may be used to save sampling costs; a stratified sample of city blocks might be selected at the first stage, then dwellings might be listed and sampled. In a large city, even if a list is available, a two-stage sample is likely to be used to save on interviewers' travel time and costs. The larger the population, the greater the number of sampling stages that are likely to be employed. A sample for a national interview survey of the U.S. population will generally employ three or more stages (see Chapter 12).

The preceding discussion has assumed for simplicity that clusters and elements were selected by SRS. In practice, stratification is used at all the stages of a multistage design for which useful stratification factors are available, and systematic sampling is also commonly used. Indeed stratification is more important for sampling clusters than for sampling elements, because it can yield much greater gains in precision when applied with clusters. In addition, many stratification factors are usually available for stratifying clusters. Stratification of the first-stage clusters, or *primary sampling units* (PSUs), in a multistage design is frequently taken to the limit of forming as many strata as there are PSUs to be sampled, and then selecting one PSU from each stratum (or implicit stratum if systematic sampling from an ordered list is used). Sometimes the sample of PSUs is further controlled by the technique of controlled selection (Goodman and Kish, 1950; Hess et al., 1975).

When a single PSU is selected from a stratum, the variance within the stratum cannot be directly estimated. To permit the estimation of sampling errors, pairs of similar strata are commonly combined and treated as if each pair constituted a single larger stratum. This *collapsed strata* technique leads to some overestimation of sampling errors, but providing the paired strata are closely similar, the overestimation should not be serious. The collapsing of pairs of strata, each with a single primary selection, sets up a design with two sampled PSUs in each stratum, a design commonly known as a *paired selection design*. The PSUs in the collapsed strata are usually treated as having been sampled with replacement so that the simple with-replacement variance estimators described earlier can be used.

6. PROBABILITY PROPORTIONAL TO SIZE SAMPLING

The last section assumed that the clusters were of equal size, but this is rarely so in practice. The natural groupings that the sampler takes advantage of to serve as clusters almost always vary in size, often in a major way. The classes in a high school will not all contain 24 students, but may perhaps vary between 20 and 30; city blocks vary much more in the number of households they contain, as also do counties (which are frequently used as PSUs for national samples in the United States). The difficulties this variation in size creates will now be explained and methods will be described by which these difficulties can be overcome.

For ease of exposition we will use an artificially small example involving the selection of an epsem sample of dwellings (the elements) from a set of 9 city blocks (the PSUs); the example might be thought of as one stratum in a much larger design. The 9 blocks contain 315 dwellings in total, and a sample of 21 is desired, implying an overall sampling fraction of 1 in 15. At the first stage of sampling, 3 blocks are to be drawn, and then dwellings are sampled within the selected blocks. Initially we assume that the sizes of the blocks—i.e., the numbers of dwellings they contain—are known without error. These sizes, with B_α denoting the number of dwellings in block α, are as follows:

Block:	1	2	3	4	5	6	7	8	9	Total
B_α:	20	100	50	15	18	43	20	36	13	315

The first design to be considered takes an SRS of three blocks at the first stage. Each block thus has a probability of $3/9 = 1/3$ of being selected. The selection probability for a dwelling can be obtained using the multiplication rule of probabilities. In general, with a two-stage design the probability of element β in cluster α appearing in the sample is

$$P(\alpha\beta) = P(\alpha)P(\beta|\alpha) \qquad [19]$$

where $P(\alpha)$ is the probability of cluster α being selected, and $P(\beta|\alpha)$ is the probability of element β in cluster α being chosen at the second stage, given that cluster α was selected at the first stage. This equation, which can be extended to cover more sampling stages when necessary, is sometimes known as the *selection equation* in the survey sampling literature.

The current example requires an overall epsem design with $f = P(\alpha\beta) = 1/15$. With the clusters being selected with equal probabilities, $P(\alpha) = 1/3$, it then follows from the selection equation that $P(\beta|\alpha) = 1/5$. In other words, the sampling rate at the second stage within each selected block is $1/5$. Consider now some possible samples that could arise from this sample design. At one extreme the sampled blocks could comprise the three smallest blocks—4, 5, and 9—while at the other extreme they could comprise the three largest blocks—2, 3, and 6. In the former case, the application of the 1 in 5 sampling fraction within the sampled blocks would yield a total sample of about 9 dwellings, and in the latter case it would yield a total sample of about 39. On average, over all possible simple random samples of three blocks that could be selected, the sample size is 21, but the actual sample size achieved in a single application may deviate substantially from this figure.

The substantial variability in possible sample size in this example is partially accounted for by the unrealistically small sample of clusters being taken. On the other hand, in other sampling problems the variability in cluster sizes may be much greater than in the blocks considered here. It is clear that some control on the potential variability in sample size is needed. While the sample size rarely needs to be specified exactly, it does need to be kept within reasonable bounds.

One way to reduce the potential variability in sample size is to stratify the clusters by size. In this example the blocks could be divided into three strata according to size: One stratum would contain blocks 2, 3, and 6, the second would contain blocks 1, 7, and 8, and the third blocks 4, 5, and 9. Selecting one block from each stratum would reduce the variability in sample size to extremes from about 15 (blocks 1 or 7, 6, and 9) to 31 (blocks 2, 5, and 8). With a larger number of selections, stratification by size usually achieves adequate control on sample size. However, the use of size stratification reduces the amount of use that can be made of other stratification factors. For this reason, an alternative procedure for controlling sample size, now to be described, is generally preferred.

Let us specify the conditions that we would like the sample to satisfy in the example: (1) It should be an epsem sample, (2) it should be restricted to three blocks, and (3) the sample size should ideally be fixed at n = 21, no matter which blocks are selected. The first and third conditions imply that $P(\alpha\beta) = 1/15$ in the selection equation. The second and third conditions are met if a sample of 7 dwellings is selected from each of three selected blocks, irrespective of the blocks' sizes; if this is done, the selection probability at the second stage in sampled block α is $P(\beta|\alpha) = 7/B_\alpha$. Substituting $P(\alpha\beta) = 1/15$ and $P(\beta|\alpha) = 7/B_\alpha$ in the selection equation gives

$$\frac{1}{15} = P(\alpha) \cdot \frac{7}{B_\alpha}$$

which may be solved to give the probability of selection of block α as $P(\alpha) = B_\alpha/105$. Thus, all three conditions are met if the blocks are sampled with probability proportional to their B_α's, i.e., with *probability proportional to size* (PPS).

In general, the selection equation for an epsem two-stage sample with PPS selection is given by

$$P(\alpha\beta) = f = \frac{n}{N} = \left(\frac{aB_\alpha}{\Sigma B_\alpha}\right)\left(\frac{b}{B_\alpha}\right) \qquad [20]$$

where $\underline{a}$ PSUs are selected by PPS, b elements are sampled from each selected PSU, n = ab, and $N = \Sigma B_\alpha$. The equation can be extended to a three-stage design, with $\underline{a}$ PSUs selected, b second stage units (SSUs) sampled within each selected PSU, and c elements sampled within each SSU as

$$P(\alpha\beta\gamma) = f = \frac{n}{N} = \left(\frac{aB_\alpha}{\Sigma B_\alpha}\right)\left(\frac{bB_{\alpha\beta}}{B_\alpha}\right)\left(\frac{c}{B_{\alpha\beta}}\right)$$

where now n = abc, $B_{\alpha\beta}$ is the size of SSU β in PSU α, and $\underset{\beta}{\Sigma} B_{\alpha\beta} = B_\alpha$.

The selection of the blocks with PPS can be achieved by cumulating their sizes as follows:

Block:	1	2	3	4	5	6	7	8	9
B_α:	20	100	50	15	18	43	20	36	13
Cumulative B_α:	20	120	170	185	203	246	266	302	315

Using the cumulative totals, numbers are associated with each block: Block 1 is allocated the 20 numbers from 001 to 020; block 2 the 100 numbers from 021 to 120; block 3 the 50 numbers from 121 to 170; and so on. In this way each block is assigned as many numbers as its size B_α. A random number chosen from 001 to 315 then selects a block with PPS. If the random number were, say 197, block 5 would be selected.

Three random numbers could be drawn in the manner outlined above to give the required 3 sampled blocks, but this with-replacement sampling scheme gives a block a chance of being selected more than once. Systematic sampling can be used to give a simple without-replacement PPS sampling method. The total size, 315, is divided by the number of selections to be made—3—to give the sampling interval of 105. A random number up to 105 is chosen, say 047, to determine the first selection, block 2. Then 105 is added to the random number to give 152, making block 3 the second selection; adding 105 again gives 257, making block 7 the third selection.

The ultimate cluster sampling approximation described in the last section can also be used with a PPS design. Suppose that at the second stage of the PPS design the b elements sampled from each selected PSU are drawn by SRS. Then, for the matching ultimate cluster design, within each of the population's PSUs the UCs can be formed as before, taking b elements by SRS to comprise the first UC, taking b elements by SRS from the remainder to comprise the second UC, and so on until all the elements are accounted for. In this way PSU α with B_α elements is divided into B_α/b UCs. (We assume for simplicity that B_α/b is an integer.) An SRS of a UCs is then equivalent to the PPS without replacement design, except that the ultimate cluster design may select more than one UC from a PSU, whereas this is not possible with the PPS design. Providing the chance of choosing two UCs from the same PSU is small with the ultimate cluster sample, the difference between the two designs is negligible. The similarity between the two designs can be seen by noting that with the ultimate cluster design the probability of sampling a UC from PSU α is proportional to the PSU's number of UCs, B_α/b (i.e., is proportional to the PSU's size).

Since the PPS design is epsem and has a fixed sample size, the simple sample mean

$$\bar{y}_p = \sum_\alpha \sum_\beta y_{\alpha\beta}/n = \sum_\alpha \bar{y}_\alpha/a$$

is an unbiased estimator of the population mean. The ultimate cluster sample approximation gives a variance estimator for $V(\bar{y}_p)$ from formula 16, ignoring the fpc term, as

$$v(\bar{y}_p) \doteq s_a^2/a \qquad [21]$$

Also, the approximate design effect for the sample mean based on a PPS design at the first stage and SRS at the second stage is given by formula 17, namely $[1 + (b - 1)\rho]$.

In practice, PPS sampling as described is seldom possible, because the true sizes of the sampling units are usually unknown. Often, however, good estimates are available from a recent census or some other source, and on other occasions reasonable estimates may be made by other means. Providing the estimated sizes, or measures of size, are reasonably good, their use in place of true sizes in a PPS selection procedure can serve well. It is, however, important to distinguish between the use of true sizes and estimated sizes; we will therefore reserve the term "probability proportional to size" (PPS) sampling for cases in which true sizes are employed, and will use the term "probability proportional to estimated size" (PPES) sampling for other cases. Estimated sizes, or measures of size, will be denoted by M_α.

Corresponding to formula 20, the selection equation for a two-stage PPES design with $\underline{a}$ PSUs selected at the first stage is

$$P(\alpha\beta) = f = \left(\frac{aM_\alpha}{\Sigma M_\alpha}\right)\left(\frac{b}{M_\alpha}\right) \qquad [22]$$

An important implication of this equation is that, in order for the sample to be an epsem one, the sampling rate at the second stage is (b/M_α). Applying this rate to the B_α elements in selected PSU α gives an expected sample size from that PSU of $b(B_\alpha/M_\alpha)$. This expected sample size will vary from PSU to PSU depending on the ratio (B_α/M_α), and will equal the desired sample size b only when $M_\alpha = B_\alpha$, i.e., when the PSU's estimated size equals its true size. This variability in the sample taken from different PSUs has to be accepted to retain the epsem property; the variability will be tolerable, providing the estimated sizes are reasonably accurate.

As an illustration, suppose that the true sizes (B_α) of the nine blocks in the earlier example were not known. A rapid tour of the area provides some rough estimates M_α that are used in a PPES selection. The values of M_α are given below, with the expected sample sizes from each PSU, assuming that the PSU was selected. These expected sample sizes are calculated by applying the subsampling rate $7/M_\alpha$ to the B_α elements in the cluster taken from the earlier figures. Once selected, the true size of a PSU would be determined.

Block:	1	2	3	4	5	6	7	8	9
M_α:	30	110	50	20	20	50	10	50	20
B_α:	20	100	50	15	18	43	20	36	13
Expected sample size:	4.7	6.4	7.0	5.3	6.3	6.0	14.0	5.0	4.6

The expected sample sizes vary somewhat because of the inaccuracies in the M_α, but mostly the variability is reasonable. Notice, however, the large expected sample size from PSU 7 if selected, which occurs because that PSU's true size (20) has been substantially underestimated. In assigning measures of size, care needs to be taken to avoid gross underestimation, because of the difficulties created. Consider, for instance, the situation of a block with an estimated 10 dwellings based on the last census, where a recent high-rise building has just been completed with 800 new dwellings. Another notable feature of these expected sample sizes is that most of them are below the b value of 7. The explanation for this lies in the fact that the M_α's tend to overestimate the B_α's: $\Sigma M_\alpha = 360$ compared with $\Sigma B_\alpha = 315$. With an intended total sample of $n = 21$, the overall sampling fraction was set at $21/360$; the expected total sample size is thus only $(21/360)315 = 18.4$. This discrepancy draws attention to the need for a good estimate of the total population size.

As the preceding discussion shows, a consequence of using PPES sampling is that the total sample size is not fixed, but is a random variable that depends on which PSUs are selected. To emphasize this fact, the total sample size will be represented by x rather than n, and the sample mean by $r = y/x$, where y is the sample total for the y variable. The sample mean is termed a *ratio mean* or *ratio estimator* because it is a ratio of random variables. The ratio mean is not an unbiased estimator of the population mean, but the bias is negligible when the variability in x is sufficiently small. The bias can be safely ignored when the coefficient of variation of x is less than 0.1, where the coefficient of variation is defined as the standard error of x divided by its expected value, the expected sample size.

The variance of the ratio mean is complicated by the fact that its denominator is a random variable. As a result, only a large sample approximation, based on what is sometimes called the Taylor expansion or delta method, is available. The appropriate use of this approximation requires the coefficient of variation of x to be small, less than 0.2 and preferably less than 0.1. The general form of the approximate variance estimator for the ratio mean $r = y/x$ is

$$v(r) \doteq [v(y) + r^2 v(x) - 2rc(x,y)]/x^2 \qquad [23]$$

where $c(x,y)$ is the sample covariance of x and y. In applying this formula, appropriate formulae need to be substituted for $v(y)$, $v(x)$, and $c(x,y)$. As an illustration, consider an epsem stratified multistage design. Let $y_{h\alpha}$ be the sample total of the y variable for PSU α in stratum h, let $x_{h\alpha}$ be the sample size in that PSU, let y_h be the total of the y variable for the a_h sampled PSUs in stratum h, and let x_h be the sample size in that stratum. Then, using the with-replacement approximation,

$$v(y) = \sum_h a_h s_{yh}^2$$

$$v(x) = \sum_h a_h s^2_{xh}$$

$$c(x, y) = \sum_h a_h s_{xyh}$$

where

$$s^2_{yh} = \sum_\alpha [y_{h\alpha} - (y_h/a_h)]^2/(a_h - 1)$$

$$s^2_{xh} = \sum_\alpha [x_{h\alpha} - (x_h/a_h)]^2/(a_h - 1)$$

$$s_{xyh} = \sum_\alpha [x_{h\alpha} - (x_h/a_h)] \ [y_{h\alpha} - (y_h/a_h)]/(a_h - 1)$$

The generality of $v(r)$ in formula 23 with the above substitutions deserves note. The formula applies to *any* epsem stratified multistage design. It applies no matter what probabilities are used for selecting the PSUs and no matter what form of subsampling is employed within selected PSUs. The formula applies to samples in which a nonstratified selection of PSUs is taken (as the special case with only one stratum) and to PPS samples where the sample size is fixed—when $v(x) = 0$ and $c(x,y) = 0$. It can be applied to ratio means and percentages based on the total sample and on subclasses (e.g., wage earners or married persons only). The only restrictions are the need for the coefficient of variation to be less than 0.2, and the need for the with-replacement approximation to be suitable. By modifying the definitions of y_α and x_α, formula 23 can be readily extended to apply to nonepsem designs. See Kish (1965: chap. 6) for further discussion.

Before leaving the subject of PPS and PPES sampling, one further illustration will be given to draw attention to some difficulties that are often met in practice. For this purpose, the earlier example of sampling dwellings from three blocks is modified as follows. The three blocks are now to be selected from ten with the following estimated sizes, M_α, with $\Sigma M_\alpha = 315$:

Block:	1	2	3	4	5	6	7	8	9	10
M_α:	20	120	45	15	18	43	5	0	36	13

As before, the desired sample size is 21, implying a desired subsample size of $b = 7$. There are two problems with applying the previous selection procedures to this population.

In the first place, the use of systematic sampling with an interval of 105 could lead to block 2 being selected twice. Since its size is greater than the interval, it is bound to appear once in the sample, and it has a probability of $15/105 = 1/7$ of being chosen twice: if the random start lies between 021 and 035, PSU 2 will be selected as the first selection and also as the second selection, since adding 105 to a number in this range gives a number no greater than 140, the upper number associated with block 2 in the cumulative totals. One solution is simply to accept the two selections if they occur, taking two different subsamples from the block. Another solution is to note that PSU 2 is bound to appear and is thus, in effect, a stratum. It is then set aside as a separate stratum and its elements are sampled at the overall sampling rate, here 1 in 15. Two selections are then made from the remaining blocks with PPES, also at the overall rate of $1/15$. A reduction in the value of b is needed since now with 2 selections from a stratum with $\Sigma M_\alpha = 195$, $2b/195 = 1/15$, i.e., $b = 6.5$. PSUs that are large enough to be certain to appear at least once in the sample occur very often in practice. They are frequently treated as separate strata and are termed, misleadingly, self-representing PSUs.

The overlarge PSUs are identified in the selection equation as those with first-stage selection probabilities greater than 1; in the case of block 2 its selection probability is $aM_\alpha/\Sigma M_\alpha = (3 \times 120/315) = 360/315$. The other commonly encountered problem with PPS or PPES selections is undersized PSUs, which give rise to second-stage selection probabilities b/M_α in excess of 1. Block 7 falls in this category in the current example since $b = 6.5$ and its measure of size is only 5. One simple way to handle this problem is to link the block to a geographically adjacent one, and treat the two as one cluster. This can be done in any convenient way before the selections are made, or afterward if objective linking rules are used (see Kish, 1965: 244-245). If there are many undersized PSUs and linking would cause fieldwork difficulties, they may be placed in a separate stratum and sampled differently. Often the minimum PSU size is set larger than b in order to avoid the possible contamination effects in data collection that could arise from sampling all (or a high proportion) of elements in the PSU. With b = 6.5, a minimum PSU size of 13, for instance, ensures that no subsampling rate exceeds 1/2.

Finally, note that $M_\alpha = 0$ for block 8, which therefore has no chance of being selected into the sample. Since, however, M_α is only an estimated size, perhaps being out of date, block 8 may now contain some dwellings. A linkage of block 8 to an adjacent block is advisable to give any dwellings now in block 8 a chance of selection. The use of this linkage avoids the bias involved in having some population elements with zero probabilities of appearing in the sample. An important feature of area samples is that every piece of habitable land be given a chance of selection if the sample is to be drawn some time after the measures of size are determined.

7. OTHER PROBABILITY DESIGNS

In combination, the sampling methods discussed in the previous chapters are sufficient to handle most sampling problems. There are, however, three other design features that are applicable in certain circumstances and deserve some attention: two-phase sampling, replicated sampling and panel designs. These three designs are reviewed in this chapter.

Two-Phase Sampling

In two-phase, or double, sampling, certain items of information are collected for an initial, or first-phase, sample, then further items are collected at the second phase from a subsample of the initial sample. The method may be extended to more phases (multiphase sampling), but for most purposes two phases suffice.

One use for two-phase sampling arises when the levels of precision needed for different estimates from a survey are not compatible, implying that different sample sizes would be appropriate. In this situation the information required to form the estimates needing the larger sample could be obtained from the first-phase sample, and that required to form the other estimates could be obtained only from the second-phase sample. Not only does this two-phase procedure have the potential for saving data collection and processing costs, it also reduces the burden placed on some respondents. A familiar example of the use of two-phase sampling in this way is provided by the U.S. Census of Population and Housing. In recent censuses, basic demographic and other variables have been collected for the total population (the first-phase sample thus being a complete enumeration), while additional variables have been collected only for samples of the population.

Other uses of two-phase sampling arise when the sample designer would like to use certain population data to produce an efficient design, but when the expense of obtaining those data for all the population would be too great. In such cases, it may sometimes be economical to collect the data for a large first-phase sample, and then to use them in selecting the second-phase sample. The first-phase sample may be used in this way to provide stratification information, size measures for PPS or PPES selection, or clustering for economies of data collection for the second-phase sample. In assessing the efficiency of a two-phase design, the costs of conducting the first-phase survey have to be recognized; because of these costs, the second-phase sample size is necessarily smaller than a single-phase sample. For this reason, two-phase designs are usually helpful only when the first-phase element survey costs are smaller than those for the second phase by a large factor. Sufficiently large differences between first- and second-phase costs can occur when different data collection procedures are used—perhaps data taken from records, or collected by mail or telephone for the first phase, and then face-to-face interviews or expensive measurements taken (as in some medical surveys) at the second phase.

Two-phase sampling is often used for sampling rare populations—that is, subgroups of the population for which no separate sampling frame exists, such as Vietnam veterans, blacks, and the recently retired. The design of good, economical, probability samples for rare populations is one of the most challenging tasks the survey sampler faces (see Kish, 1965: section 11.4). One technique to consider is a two-phase design in which the first-phase sample identifies the members of the rare population inexpensively, and the survey items are then collected from them at the second phase. In essence, the approach involves the use of two-phase stratified sampling. The members of the first-phase sample are allocated into two (or more) strata according to whether they are members of the rare population or not. The strata are then sampled disproportionately. If the first-phase identification of the rare population is error-free, then the sampling rates may be set at 1 for the stratum of members and at 0 for the stratum of nonmembers of the rare population. If the identification is subject to error, however, the sampling rate in the second stratum needs to be nonzero in order to give members of the rare population falsely allocated to that stratum some chance of being selected. When the first-phase screening is imperfect it is preferable, where possible, to err in favor of false positives rather than false negatives, since the former can be handled more easily. Thus, for example, in a study of severe hearing loss among children, the initial home-based screening used a less stringent definition of hearing loss with the aim of ensuring that all children with severe hearing loss were included in the second phase of the study, which involved measurements made under controlled laboratory conditions.

An illustration of the use of two-phase sampling for clustering comes from a survey of political attitudes among electors in a European city. An alphabetical list of electors with their addresses was available as a sampling frame. Since the city was a large one and the survey was to be conducted by face-to-face interviewing, some clustering of the sample was desired to reduce interviewers' travel costs. In theory, the electors' addresses could have been used to allocate the whole of the electorate to clusters, but that would have been prohibitively expensive. Instead, a sample of electors ten times larger than required was selected, this sample was allocated to clusters of equal size based on geographical proximity, and then one-tenth of the clusters were selected to comprise the final sample.

Replicated Sampling

In replicated, or interpenetrating, sampling, the total sample is made up of a set of replicate subsamples, each of the identical sample design. Replicated sampling may be used for studying variable nonsampling errors, such as the variability in the results obtained by different interviewers and coders, and for facilitating the calculation of standard errors. The essential feature for either use is that each subsample provides independent comparable estimates of the population parameters.

As a simple example of the use of replicated sampling for studying variable interviewer effects, suppose that an SRS of 1000 is required, with a team of 20 interviewers conducting the fieldwork. With an unreplicated design, the sample of 1000 would be selected and allocated between interviewers on grounds of general convenience and geographical proximity, perhaps with interviews in the more difficult areas being assigned to the best interviewers. When one interviewer failed to secure a response, the interview might be reissued to a more experienced interviewer. As a result of this nonrandom assignment of interviewers, differences in interviewers' results may arise from interviewer effects, from differences in the subsamples they interview, or from both; these two sources of differences are confounded and cannot be disentangled.

For a simple replicated design, the sample of 1000 could be selected as 20 independent SRSs, each of size 50, with each interviewer then being responsible for obtaining the 50 interviews in one of the replicates. Since the replicates are comparable samples, any differences in the subsample results beyond those likely to arise from sampling fluctuations can be attributed to systematic differences between interviewers in the responses they obtain. The approach employed for distinguishing between sampling fluctuations and real differences is that used in a standard one-way analysis of variance (see, for instance, Iversen and Norpoth, 1976); however, the calculations are different when the replicates employ complex sample designs.

To describe the calculations of interviewer variance, let $\bar{y}_1, \bar{y}_2, \ldots \bar{y}_c$ denote the means obtained from the c subsamples allocated to the different interviewers. The variance of these c means may be estimated by $v_1 = \Sigma(\bar{y}_\gamma - \bar{y})^2/(c - 1)$ where $\bar{y} = \Sigma\bar{y}_\gamma/c$ is the mean of the sample means. This estimator makes no assumption about the presence or absence of systematic interviewer effects; when they are present, the estimator will be expected to be larger than when they are absent. Under the null hypothesis of no interviewer effects, SRS theory can be used to provide another estimator of the variance of the $\bar{y}_\gamma$'s: Ignoring the fpc term, $v(\bar{y}_\gamma) = s_\gamma^2/r$ from formula 3 where s_γ^2 is the estimated element variance in the γth subsample, and $r = n/c$ is the subsample size. An average of the estimates of $v(\bar{y}_\gamma)$ across the c subsamples is given by $v_2 = \bar{s}^2/r$, where $\bar{s}^2 = \Sigma s_\gamma^2/c$ is the average of the within-subsample element variance estimates. Comparison of v_1 and v_2 then provides a test of the null hypothesis. This comparison is made by taking the ratio $F = v_1/v_2 = r v_1/\bar{s}^2$, with a large value of F indicating the presence of interviewer variance. The significance test for F greater than 1 is obtained using a standard F-test with $(c - 1)$ and $c(r - 1) = (n - c)$ degrees of freedom. A useful index of interviewer variance is the intraclass correlation coefficient ρ, measuring the proportion of the total variance in the y-values that is accounted for by interviewer variance. The value of ρ may be estimated by $(F - 1)/(F - 1 + r)$. See Kish (1962) for an example.

The consequences of variation among interviewers are similar to those of clustering; each interviewer's assignment is in effect a separate cluster. Thus, equivalent to the design effect for a cluster sample, the effect of interviewer variance for the replicated design described above is to multiply the SRS variance of the overall sample mean by $[1 + (r - 1)\rho]$. As with clustering, even a small value of ρ leads to a sizable multiplier if r—the number of interviews conducted by each interviewer—is large. The usual estimator of the variance of the overall mean from SRS theory (formula 3) does not allow for the effects of clustering or of interviewer variance. An attraction of the replicated sampling variance estimator based on the variation between subsamples is that it automatically encompasses the clustering effect of interviewer variance. As shown below, this variance estimator is in fact v_1/c, which is simply the standard cluster sampling variance estimator, s_a^2/a, from formula 15 in a different guise.

The cost of using replicated sampling to study systematic interviewer effects, or interviewer variance, comes from the need to give interviewers randomly chosen, rather than the most efficient, assignments. The ease of conducting interviewer variance studies depends on the general survey conditions; they are, for instance, much more readily incorporated into telephone than face-to-face surveys, and in face-to-face surveys they are simpler to conduct with small, compact populations. A completely random assignment of interviews across a multistage sample of a widely dispersed population would clearly create excessive interviewer travel costs, but completely random assignments are not required. Some form of restricted replication—for instance, random interviewer assignments within PSUs or strata—can still permit the estimation of interviewer variance.

The second use of replicated sampling, to provide simple variance estimates, employs much the same reasoning as above. Given c estimates $z_1, z_2, \ldots z_c$ of parameter Z, obtained from independent replicates of the same design, the variance of the mean of the estimates $\bar{z} = \Sigma z_\gamma/c$ is given by

$$V(\bar{z}) = V(z_\gamma)/c$$

and $V(z_\gamma)$ may be estimated from the c values as

$$v_1 = \Sigma(z_\gamma - \bar{z})^2/(c - 1)$$

Thus

$$v(\bar{z}) = v_1/c = \Sigma(z_\gamma - \bar{z})^2/c(c - 1) \qquad [24]$$

provides a general formula for estimating variances from replicated designs. It can be applied to any form of statistic (such as index numbers, correlation and regression coefficients, as well as simple means and percentages), and the subsample design can be of any complex form (such as a stratified multistage PPS design).

A small problem with the use of formula 24 is that it gives the variance of the average of the replicate values $\bar{z}$. This average value is not in general the same as the estimator obtained by pooling the subsamples into one large sample, $\tilde{z}$, and $\tilde{z}$ is as a rule the preferred estimator. In practice, however, the difference between $\bar{z}$ and $\tilde{z}$ is usually slight. A commonly adopted procedure is to compute $\tilde{z}$ and use $v(\bar{z})$ from formula 24, or a slight variant of it, to provide a variance estimate for $\tilde{z}$.

A more serious problem centers on the choice of c, the number of replicates to be employed. If a small value of c is chosen, the replicated variance estimator $v(\bar{z})$ will be imprecise, and this imprecision will affect the width of the confidence interval for the parameter being estimated. With c replicates, $v(\bar{z})$ has $(c - 1)$ degrees of freedom; hence, in forming confidence intervals, the t distribution with $(c - 1)$ degrees of freedom should be employed. As an illustration of this effect, consider an SRS of 1000 elements. The 95% confidence interval for $\bar{Y}$ obtained from the conventional approach is $\bar{y} \pm 1.96 s / \sqrt{n}$, where 1.96 is taken from a table for the normal distribution. With a replicated design with 10 subsamples of 100 each, the 95% confidence interval is $\bar{y} \pm 2.26 \sqrt{v_1 / 10}$, where 2.26 is taken from a table for the t distribution with 9 degrees of freedom. With a replicated design with 4 subsamples of 250 each, the 95% confidence interval is $\bar{y} \pm 3.18 \sqrt{v_1 / 4}$, where 3.18 comes from a table for the t distribution with 3 degrees of freedom. Since in each case the standard error estimator is unbiased for the true variance of $\bar{y}$, the replicated variance estimator with 10 replicates leads to a confidence interval that is on average 15% larger, and that with 4 replicates to a confidence interval that is on average 62% larger, than that based on the conventional variance estimator. To obtain a reasonably precise variance estimator, a relatively large value of c is needed, perhaps around 20 to 30 or more. On the other hand, the greater the value of c, the less stratification that can be employed. This situation occurs because each subsample must take at least one selection from each stratum. The restriction on stratification is especially harmful with multistage designs. As an illustration, suppose that 60 PSUs are selected. With a conventional design, the PSUs would probably be divided into 60 strata with one selection per stratum, or perhaps 30 strata with two selections per stratum. With a replicated design with 10 replicates, the maximum number of strata is reduced to only 6.

In summary, the benefit of a simple and general variance estimator with replicated sampling is bought at the cost of some loss of precision: Either c is small and the precision of the variance estimator suffers from limited degrees of freedom, or c is large and the precision of the survey estimator itself suffers through the loss of stratification. For these reasons, simple replicated sampling as described is not greatly used in practice. Instead, pseudoreplication techniques have been developed to enable stratification to be employed to the point of the paired selection design, yet also to give variance estimates of reasonable precision. These techniques are described in Chapter 10.

Panel Designs

It has been implicitly assumed thus far that the samples are being designed for cross-sectional surveys with one round of data collection. There are, however, many survey objectives that require data to be collected at two or more points of time. While the preceding sample designs remain applicable, some additional sampling considerations arise when the time dimension is included.

One purpose of several rounds of data collection is to measure changes over time. An important distinction needs to be made here between gross and net changes, the former referring to changes at the element level and the latter to changes in the aggregate. If measures of individual changes are needed—as for example in a study to examine in detail the effects of changing leisure activities on blood pressures—then the data must be collected for the same sampled elements on each round. If only net changes are required—as perhaps in a study to chart the changes in popularity of a political leader—then the data do not have to be collected from the same elements. Even with net changes, however, it may be more efficient to retain the same sample.

Another purpose of conducting surveys at several points of time is to collect information when it is readily accessible and can be reported accurately. Thus, for instance, in a survey requiring a detailed accounting of annual household incomes, several interviews may be taken during the course of the year in order to collect information while it is fresh in the respondents' minds. Again, a study investigating the association between children's preschool upbringing and school performance would almost certainly need to collect data on preschool upbringing as it takes place and then later collect data on school performance. It would be unsafe to rely on retrospective reports of preschool training, because it would be imperfectly remembered and because the memory may be distorted by the results of school performance.

A panel or longitudinal survey, in which data are collected from the same sampled elements on more than one occasion, raises some further issues in addition to those applying with a cross-sectional survey. One issue is the mobility of the sampled elements. In most panel surveys, some of the elements—often persons or households—will move during the life of the panel. These movers need to be retained in the panel in order to keep intact the probability sample selected at the start, and this requires the development of effective tracing methods. Since some movers will leave the sampled PSUs of a multistage design, mobility will cause an increase in data collection costs for later rounds of a survey employing face-to-face interviewing.

A second issue that needs to be faced with panel surveys is that populations change over time; some elements in the original population leave while others enter. Consider, for example, a long-term panel survey of the health of a particular community. At the start, a probability sample of members of the community is drawn, and they are followed for several years. During this time the community's population will change: Some of the original members will leave, through death or because they move out of the community, while new members will enter—births and movers into the community. The main problem created by leavers is the reduction in sample size; the panel remains a probability sample of that part of the orginal population that still lives in the community. The problem with entrants, on the other hand, is that they are not represented in the sample. In consequence, the sample is not a probability sample of all the community's population as it exists at later rounds of data collection. When a population has a significant proportion of new entrants and when cross-sectional results are needed for the population present at a later round, a supplement sample of entrants is needed. An added complexity occurs when the element of analysis is a grouping such as a household or family. A sizable proportion of households or families is likely to change composition over even such a short period as a year, creating severe conceptual and practical problems in a panel survey.

Another concern with panel surveys is that repeated interviewing may have adverse effects on respondents. Some may object to the burden and refuse to remain in the panel, thus causing a bias in the panel membership (see Chapter 9 on nonresponse). Others may be influenced by their panel membership with regard to the survey's subject matter so that they give untypical responses. This panel conditioning effect can, for instance, occur in consumer panels in which respondents are asked to report their household purchases on a regular basis. The act of reporting can make respondents more price conscious; hence they may alter their patterns of purchases. A related risk in a panel study asking for the same information repeatedly is that respondents may remember their previous responses and attempt to give consistent answers.

A widely used method to alleviate some of the problems of panels is to limit the length of panel membership by using some form of panel rotation. As a simple example, each member of the panel might be retained for three rounds of the survey. For each round, one-third of the sample from the previous round would be dropped, and a new one-third would be added: the new third would be included also in the following two rounds. Thus, using letters to represent the three parts of the sample, the first round sample is, say ABC, the second round BCD, the third round CDE, the fourth round DEF, and so on. In this way there is a two-thirds overlap in sample membership between adjacent rounds and a one-third overlap between rounds that are one round apart.

As observed earlier, a panel design may be useful but is not essential for estimating net change. Consider the simple estimator $\bar{y}_2 - \bar{y}_1$ of the change in mean level of variable y between times 1 and 2. The variance of this difference is given in general by

$$V(\bar{y}_2 - \bar{y}_1) = V(\bar{y}_1) + V(\bar{y}_2) - 2\bar{R}\sqrt{V(\bar{y}_1)\,V(\bar{y}_2)} \qquad [25]$$

where $\bar{R}$ is the product-moment correlation coefficient between the sample means $\bar{y}_1$ and $\bar{y}_2$. With independent samples on the two rounds of the survey, $\bar{R} = 0$. With overlapping samples $\bar{R}$ is not 0; it is generally positive, but on occasion it can be negative. The last term in formula 25 reflects the gains ($\bar{R}$ positive) or losses ($\bar{R}$ negative) in the precision of the estimator of change through using a panel design.

To obtain further insight into the effect of sample overlap on the measurement of change, consider the simple case of a static population and simple random sampling with a sample of size of n on each occasion; furthermore, assume—as is often a reasonable approximation—that the element variances on the two occasions are equal (i.e., $S_1^2 = S_2^2 = S^2$), and ignore the fpc term. Then, with a partial overlap of a proportion P in the two samples, the general formula 25 reduces to

$$V(\bar{y}_2 - \bar{y}_1) = 2S^2(1 - PR)/n$$

where R is the correlation between the elements' y values on the two occasions. The situations of independent samples and of complete overlap are special cases of this formula, the first with P = 0 and the second with P = 1. When P = 0, the variance of the difference is simply $2S^2/n$, so that the ratio of the variance of the difference with a panel design to that with two independent samples is $(1 - PR)$. As an illustration, suppose that the correlation in individuals' political attitudes (or perhaps blood pressures) for the two occasions is 0.75. Then the completely overlapping panel would reduce the variance of $\bar{y}_2 - \bar{y}_1$ by a multiplying factor of $(1 - 0.75) = 0.25$. A partial overlap of two-thirds (rotating out one-third) would reduce the variance by a factor of $[1 - (0.75 \times 2/3)] = 0.50$. If the correlations across time are high, the gains of the panel design in measuring change are thus considerable. In the case of a rotating panel design, further gains can be achieved by using a more complex estimator of the change (see Kish, 1965: 463-464). Note, however, that if R is negative—as would occur if the y variable were the purchase of a consumer durable in the last month—then the panel design leads to a loss of precision in measuring change. If, say, $R = -0.2$, and with complete overlap $P = 1$, then $(1 - PR) = 1.2$, so that the variance of the change is 20% larger with the panel design than with two independent samples.

Finally, we should note that the gains from positive correlations in nonindependent samples shown in formula 25 are not confined to the situation where the same elements are kept in a panel. Designs that retain the same clusters but select different elements can also be helpful for measuring changes, although the degree of correlation $\bar{R}$ will generally be less than that occurring when the same elements are retained. A useful design for avoiding the need to follow movers is to sample dwellings rather than households; a household moving out of a sampled dwelling is then replaced in the panel by the incoming household.

8. SAMPLING FRAMES

The sampling frame is a major ingredient of the overall sample design. At minimum it provides a means of identifying and locating the population elements, and it usually contains a good deal of additional information that can be used for stratification and clustering. The organization of the frame also often exerts a strong influence on the sample design. Areal clustering is, for instance, greatly assisted by having a frame arranged in suitable geographical units, and stratification is helped by having a frame separated into groups formed by the relevant stratification factors. Frequently listed frames are stored in computer files, with the considerable benefit that they can be readily rearranged to meet sampling requirements.

The ideal sampling frame would list each population element once and once only, and would contain no other listings. In practice this ideal is seldom realized, and the survey sampler has to be on the lookout for imperfections. Kish (1965: 53-59) provided a useful fourfold classification of potential frame problems and possible solutions. The four problems are

—*missing elements:* when some population elements are not included on the frame;

—*clusters:* when some listings refer to groups of elements, not to individual elements;

—*blanks* or *foreign elements:* when some listings do not relate to elements of the survey population;

—*duplicate listings:* when some population elements have more than one listing.

These problems and their solutions are discussed and illustrated below.

Missing Elements

With the student survey we assumed the existence of a list of the school's students. The first question to be asked about this frame is whether it includes all the students in the target population. Missing elements may occur because a frame is *inadequate,* meaning that it is not intended to cover the whole of the target population, or because it is *incomplete,* meaning that it fails to include some elements from the target population that it is supposed to cover. The distinction between inadequacy and incompleteness is of practical importance because the former category is often more easily recognized. The school list would be inadequate if it deliberately excluded part-time students who are part of the target population; it would be incomplete if it was out-of-date and hence failed to include some new students.

Missing elements present the most serious frame problem because, unless a remedy is found, these elements have no chance of being selected for the sample, which thus fails to represent the total target population. Sometimes the problem may be sidestepped by defining the survey population to exclude the missing elements. This imperfect solution is often used when the excluded group is a negligible proportion of the total population, when the exclusion will have only minimal effect on the survey objectives, and when no simple alternative solution is available. A preferable solution is to find supplementary frames to cover the missing elements, for instance, lists of special students and new entrants. This solution can create the problem of duplicates because some elements may appear on more than one list, but this lesser problem may be handled by one of the methods discussed below.

Often no suitable supplementary frame is available for the missing elements, and then a solution involving some form of linking procedure may be sought. Linking procedures aim to attach missing elements to specified listings in a clearly defined way. When a listing is selected, its element and any missing element or elements linked to it are treated as being sampled as a cluster. Linking thus gives rise to the problem of clusters, which may be treated by one of the procedures outlined below. Suppose, in our school sample, that the sampling frame comprises alphabetical lists of the students present at the original enrollment for each of the classes. A possible linking for missing students would then be to define each listing as representing the named student together with any student missing from the class list coming after that student and before the next listed student in the alphabetical order. To cover missing students at the start of the alphabet, the list may be treated as circular; thus, any missing student coming after the last listed student or before the first listed student is linked to the last student on the list. This form of linking is an example of what is known as a *half-open interval,* a procedure that can also be applied in other contexts. One well-known application is for sampling dwellings from lists of dwellings in street order, with each side of the street being taken separately; using the half-open interval, missing dwellings may be linked to the last listed dwelling preceding them.

Clusters

As indicated above, one cause of the frame problem of listings of clusters of elements is the use of a linking solution for missing elements. Clusters also occur in other circumstances—for instance, when a sample of persons or households is required but the sampling frame is a list of dwellings. One solution is to include all the elements in the selected clusters in the sample. This solution has the benefit of giving the elements the same chance of appearing in the sample as their listings; in particular, if listings are sampled by epsem, the elements are also sampled by epsem. When the elements are households and the clusters are dwellings this solution often works well because of a combination of two features: First, most dwellings contain only one household, and when there is more than one the number is small; second, conducting interviews with more than one household in a dwelling seldom gives rise to fieldwork difficulties.

The "take-all" solution is a sample of complete clusters, and, as discussed earlier, cluster sampling leads to a large design effect when the average size of the clusters is large and when the intraclass correlation within the clusters is high. If the design effect is large, subsampling within clusters may be usefully employed to reduce its magnitude. With some types of cluster another major reason for subsampling is a concern about contamination of responses within a cluster. This concern often leads to a requirement of subsampling only one element per sampled cluster. It arises in particular in attitude surveys when the elements are persons and the clusters are households (or dwellings): If two or more respondents are interviewed in a household, the responses of later respondents may well be influenced by discussions about the contents of the interview with earlier respondents. Later respondents may also be less willing to cooperate, perhaps refusing to take part more often, because they have learned about the contents and length of the interview. When a single element is selected from a cluster (listing) containing B_α elements, each element's selection probability is $(1/B_\alpha)P(\alpha)$, where $P(\alpha)$ is the selection probability for the cluster. If the clusters are sampled by epsem, the sample of elements is nonepsem; hence weighting adjustments are needed in the survey analysis (see Chapter 10).

To avoid selection bias the sampling of elements from sampled clusters must be carried out by a strict probability mechanism. Consider the common problem of selecting one respondent from the eligible members of a household for a face-to-face interview survey. In this case it is highly desirable that the interviewer carry out the random selection during the first contact with the household so that, if the chosen respondent is available, the interview can be completed at that call. One possible procedure would be for the interviewer to list the eligible members on a numbered form, and then to select one using a table of random numbers. The serious drawback to this procedure is that it is uncheckable, with the danger that interviewers may sometimes mis-apply it in order to select available and cooperative respondents.

An alternative, widely used procedure for selecting a respondent from a household is commonly known as the *Kish selection grid*. The basis of this objective and checkable procedure is that the interviewer records the eligible household members in a clearly defined order on a numbered list, with the questionnaire containing a table from which the interviewer then reads off the number of the person selected. A con-venient unambiguous way for ordering the household members is to list them by age within sexes. Since only relative ages are needed for the ordering, it is seldom necessary to ask for exact ages; generational differences are usually sufficient to determine age orderings within sexes. As a simple illustration of the procedure, suppose that the survey is one of wage earners and that it is reasonable to assume that no household contains more than four wage earners. On a particular questionnaire, the table giving the interviewer instructions on which wage earner to interview might be as follows:

If the number of wage earners in the household is:	1	2	3	4
Interview wage earner numbered:	1	2	2	3

The numbers in the second row are varied across the questionnaires according to the scheme in Table 4.

In a one-wage-earner household, that wage earner is always selected. In a two-wage-earner household, the first listed wage earner is interviewed if the questionnaire contains Table A, B, or C, and the second wage earner is interviewed if it contains Table D, E, or F. From the second column of Table 4, which gives the proportion of the questionnaires that have a particular table, it can be seen that the proportion of questionnaires with Table A, B, or C is ½, and that with Table D, E, or F is ½. Thus, in two-wage-earner households, each of the wage earners is equally likely to be selected for the sample. In the same way, it can be seen that in three-wage-earner households each of the three is equally likely to be selected, and in four-wage-earner households each of the four is equally likely to be selected. Thus, although the selection of one wage earner from a household results in wage earners in households containing different numbers of wage earners having unequal selection probabilities, the Kish selection grid gives equal selection probabilities to all wage earners in a given household.

As described here, the procedure assumes a maximum of four wage earners per household. A larger maximum can be specified, but then more tables are needed. When sampling adults from U.S. households, a maximum of six is often taken. Kish (1965: 399) gives eight tables that can be used when this maximum is adopted. These tables provide equal probabilities for all members within households of size 1, 2, 3, 4, and 6, but the probabilities for members within households of size 5 are not exactly equal. In the few households with more than six members, some members go unrepresented. These deficiencies are sufficiently small to be of no practical importance.

If, as is often the case, the clusters are sampled with epsem, the first solution to the cluster problem—taking all elements in the selected clusters—yields an epsem sample of elements. However, this solution is often unacceptable because of the risk of contamination. The second solution—selecting one element at random from selected clusters—avoids the risk of contamination but at the cost of changing the selection

TABLE 4
Set of Six Tables for Selecting One Wage Earner from a Household

Table	Proportion of Questionnaires	If the number of wage earners in the household is			
		1	2	3	4
		Interview wage earner numbered:			
A	1/4	1	1	1	1
B	1/12	1	1	1	2
C	1/6	1	1	2	2
D	1/6	1	2	2	3
E	1/12	1	2	3	3
F	1/4	1	2	3	4

probabilities. A third solution uses two-phase sampling to take only one element per cluster and to retain an epsem sample. With this solution, a first-phase sample of clusters is selected and the elements in these clusters are listed. The second-phase sample selects elements from the list. Thus, for instance, suppose that the clusters are households, with no household containing more than six adults. A first-phase sample of households is selected to provide a list of at least six times as many adults as are needed for the survey. A systematic sample of the required number of adults would then take no more than one adult from a household.

Blanks and Foreign Elements

Blanks and foreign elements are listings for elements that no longer exist in the population (such as persons who have died or emigrated or dwellings that have been demolished) or listings for elements that are correctly on the frame but outside the scope of the survey (such as unemployed people in a survey of wage earners). For simplicity of exposition we will use the term "blanks" to cover both blanks and foreign elements.

The method of handling blanks is straightforward—simply to ignore the selection if a blank is drawn. This method has already been illustrated in the high school example, where some student numbers were blanks because the students had left the school. The major consequence of blanks on the sampling frame is that the sample size is smaller than the number of selections, since some blanks will be drawn and omitted.

This point needs to be borne in mind in determining the sampling fraction needed to generate the desired sample size. A common error with systematic sampling is to substitute the next element on the list when a blank is sampled. This procedure should be avoided since it increases the selection probability for the next element: That element would be selected either if it is selected directly or if the preceding blank is selected. With systematic sampling, the sampling interval should be repeated throughout the population, with blanks simply being dropped from the sample.

It is of practical importance to distinguish between the situation in which the blanks can be identified as such from the sampling frame and that in which they cannot be so identified. In the former case they can be deleted as they are sampled, but in the latter case they have to be contacted before they can be deleted. A sample of men from a listing of men and women may, for instance, be able to eliminate all, or nearly all, the women at the selection stage by means of their first names; but, with a survey of 40-64-year-olds it may be necessary to conduct screening interviews to determine whether selected individuals fall in the survey population. The difficult problem of sampling rare populations arises when the survey population comprises only a small fraction of the frame, and when the frame does not provide the means to identify elements in the survey population. As already noted, one way of identifying a sample of a rare population is to use a two-phase design, using a relatively cheap screening process at the first phase to identify elements in the rare population.

Duplicate Listings

Duplicate listings often arise when the sampling frame is composed of several lists, for then some elements may appear on more than one list. They also arise when the elements of analysis are groupings, such as households, and when the listings are of individual components, such as persons. The problem created by duplicates is that the elements' selection probabilities vary with their numbers of listings. One possibility is to remove the duplicates from the whole frame, but this is often not feasible. A second possibility is to employ *unique identification,* associating each element with one of its listings in a clearly defined way (e.g., the first listing, or the oldest listing) and treating the other listings for that element as blanks. This procedure is, for instance, used in sampling households from the Register of Electors in Britain. In urban areas, the electors are numbered and listed in polling district areas by street address. A sample of electors is readily taken by systematic sampling using the elector numbers. If a sampled elector is the first one listed at an address, that address is taken, while the selection of a second or subsequent elector at an address is treated as a blank. Then, handling the cluster problem by the take-all procedure, all households in the selected addresses are included in the sample.

Sometimes the organization of the sampling frame or the information it contains does not readily permit the use of unique identification. In such cases, unique identification could be applied during fieldwork, asking respondents to provide information on their listings. Generally, however, a substantial proportion of the survey costs is employed in making contact with respondents, so that it is uneconomical to reject some selections as blanks at interview. An alternative is to accept all selections and to use weighting in the analysis to adjust for the unequal selection probabilities (see Chapter 10).

9. NONRESPONSE

Probability sampling avoids selection bias by giving each element on the sampling frame a known and nonzero probability of selection. The methods for dealing with frame problems described in the last section were developed to help to eliminate, or at least reduce, biases resulting from frame deficiencies. Given a good frame, a probability sample of the population may be drawn, but there still remains the need to collect the survey data from the sampled elements. Failure to collect the survey data from some sampled elements, or nonresponse, is a major survey problem that seems to have grown in recent years as the public has become less willing to participate in surveys (see, for instance, Steeh, 1981).

The cause of concern about nonresponse is the risk that nonrespondents will differ from respondents with regard to the survey variables, in which case the survey estimates based on the respondents alone will be biased estimates of the overall population parameters. To obtain a more thorough understanding of this nonresponse bias, we will consider a simple model in which the population is divided into two groups—those who are certain to respond and those who are certain not to do so; these two groups may be thought of as the response and nonresponse strata. Since, in practice for some elements in the population, chance plays a part in determining whether they respond or not, the model is oversimplified, but it will suffice for present purposes. Also, for simplicity, we assume that the survey calls for a complete enumeration of the population. Suppose that the aim of the survey is to determine $\bar{Y}$, the total population mean. This mean may be expressed as

$$\bar{Y} = W_r\bar{Y}_r + W_m\bar{Y}_m$$

where $\bar{Y}_r$ and $\bar{Y}_m$ are the means for the response and nonresponse strata (the subscripts r for respondents and m for "missing"), and W_r and W_m are the proportions of the population in these two strata ($W_r + W_m = 1$). Since the survey fails to collect data for the nonrespondents, it produces the estimate $\bar{Y}_r$. The difference between $\bar{Y}_r$ and the population parameter being estimated, $\bar{Y}$, is

$$\begin{aligned}
\bar{Y}_r - \bar{Y} &= \bar{Y}_r - (W_r\bar{Y}_r + W_m\bar{Y}_m) \\
&= \bar{Y}_r(1 - W_r) - W_m\bar{Y}_m \\
&= W_m(\bar{Y}_r - \bar{Y}_m)
\end{aligned} \qquad [26]$$

This difference, which is the bias arising from using the respondent mean in place of the overall mean, is seen to depend on two factors: W_m, the proportion of nonrespondents in the population, and $(\bar{Y}_r - \bar{Y}_m)$, the difference between the means of respondents and nonrespondents. If the response and nonresponse strata were randomly formed, the respondent and nonrespondent means would be equal in expectation, and there would be no nonresponse bias. In practice, however, it is dangerous to assume that the missing responses are missing at random; indeed, there are often good grounds for believing otherwise. Therefore, the only way to make sure that the nonresponse bias is not sizable is to keep the nonresponse stratum sufficiently small to guarantee that when $(\bar{Y}_r - \bar{Y}_m)$ is multiplied by W_m the result cannot be large. Following this line of argument, the survey researcher needs to make strenuous efforts to minimize the amount of nonresponse.

In discussing nonresponse in surveys, it is useful to distinguish between two main levels at which it can arise: *total* (or *unit*) *nonresponse* occurs when no information is collected for a sampled element, and *item nonresponse* occurs when some but not all the information is collected. Total nonresponse is often termed simply "nonresponse." We will consider total nonresponse first and afterward turn to item nonresponse.

With interview surveys, total nonresponse can be classified into these categories: refusal to be interviewed; noncontact because the intended respondent is unavailable (not at home) or cannot be located; incapacity of the intended respondent to take part in the survey for reasons such as illness, deafness, or inability to speak the language; and even completed questionnaires being lost in transit or processing. Of these, refusals and not-at-homes are the dominant causes, with the others being of minor significance in most general population surveys. With mail surveys, a few members of the sample may send a reply to indicate their refusal to take part, in a few cases a neighbor or relative may reply to say that the intended respondent is too ill to respond, and some questionnaires may be returned by the post office as undeliverable. However, all that is known about most mail survey nonresponse is simply that the questionnaire has not been returned. The lack of response may be the result of one of several reasons, such as a definite decision to refuse, a failure to get around to completing the questionnaire, or the questionnaire's failure to reach the respondent.

A variety of procedures is used in survey design in an attempt to minimize the number of refusals, and even the choice of mode of data collection is often influenced by the relative risks of refusals with different modes. With interview surveys interviewers are carefully trained in approaches to use to avoid refusals, and they are instructed to return to conduct an interview at a time more convenient to the respondent if necessary. Attempts to persuade the sample members of the value of the survey are generally made, often supported by reference to a prestigious sponsor; good sponsorship is likely to be particularly effective with a mail survey. Assurances of anonymity and confidentiality are generally provided to eliminate any fears the respondents may have about the use of their responses. Questionnaires are usually organized to start with simple nonthreatening questions to avoid the risk that the respondent will terminate the interview when immediately faced with a taxing or embarrassing question. The proportion of refusals varies greatly, depending on the subject matter of the survey, the length of the questionnaire, and the skills of the survey research team.

Not-at-homes in interview surveys are treated by callbacks. In face-to-face surveys, interviewers are commonly instructed to make at least four callbacks if unable to contact a respondent, with the callbacks having to be made on different days and at different times of day, including some evening calls. The interviewers are also encouraged to make additional calls if they find themselves in the neighborhood. Appointments can be useful in increasing the chance of contacting a respondent at a subsequent call. Callbacks are much more readily accomplished in telephone surveys; hence the number of calls made is generally much larger than in face-to-face surveys. The comparable procedure to the callback in mail surveys is the follow-up—i.e., sending out further correspondence to those who have not replied. The follow-up is, however, not aimed at dealing with not-at-homes but simply with encouraging responses. A common strategy is to send a "reminder letter" to those who have not replied after a given period (perhaps two weeks) and then to send a further reminder with a second copy of the questionnaire to those who still have not replied after a further period. Follow-ups have proved to be a valuable means of increasing the proportion of responses to mail surveys. See Dillman (1978) on other ways of stimulating mail survey responses.

The response rate for a survey is defined as the ratio of the number of questionnaires completed for eligible elements to the number of eligible elements in the sample. While this definition might appear straightforward, some difficulties can be encountered in dealing with blank or foreign elements. According to the definition, such ineligible elements should be excluded from both the numerator and denominator of the rate, but it is not always possible to determine whether a sampled element is a not-at-home or a blank. Thus, for instance, with a random-digit-dialing telephone sample a number from which no response is obtained on repeated calls may be a nonworking or business number (a blank) or a household that is out on each call. Similarly, in a survey of youths aged 18 to 24, a sampled household from which no response is obtained may or may not contain one or more members of the survey population. In practice, such cases are often treated differently from one survey to another, thus producing noncomparable response rates. For this reason, reported response rates should be critically examined to see how they were computed.

Nowadays response rates for uncomplicated face-to-face surveys carried out by nongovernment survey organizations are about 70%-75%, with variability around this range according to the survey conditions. As a general rule, refusals constitute the majority of the nonresponses with the rest being mostly not-at-homes. Telephone surveys usually experience somewhat lower response rates than face-to-face surveys, with refusal being the dominant reason for nonresponse. Telephone surveys are also subject to "break-off" interviews, in which the respondent stops the interview before it is completed. Response rates in mail surveys are extremely varied, ranging from as low as 10% to over 90%. This variation depends in part on the efforts made with follow-ups, and on the subject of the survey and its relevance to the survey population.

At the current levels of nonresponse, the risk of nonresponse bias cannot be ignored. Moreover, there is often evidence that nonresponse is not evenly spread across the population, but is more heavily concentrated among subgroups. Nonresponse rates in face-to-face interview surveys are, for instance, commonly found to be much higher in inner cities than elsewhere. As a consequence of this differential nonresponse, the distribution of the achieved sample across the subgroups will deviate from that of the selected sample. This deviation is likely to give rise to nonresponse bias if the survey variables are also related to the subgroups. If subgroups with differential nonresponse rates can be identified, an attempt can be made to compensate for the potential nonresponse bias by weighting adjustments in the analysis, as described in the next section. It should, however, be noted that these adjustments only redress the distribution of the sample for the known imbalances, and there can be no guarantee that they will remove—or even reduce—any nonresponse bias. They eliminate nonresponse bias only when the nonrespondents are a random subset of the total sample in each subgroup with regard to the survey variables—an unlikely occurrence in practice. Thus, although weighting adjustments may go some way toward compensating for nonresponse, they do not provide a full solution to the problem. The use of weighting adjustments in the analyses does not obviate the need for strenuous efforts to secure a high response rate in data collection.

Item nonresponse, which is evidenced by inappropriate gaps in the data records for responding elements, may occur for a variety of reasons. Survey informants may not know the answers to certain questions or they may refuse to answer some questions because they find them sensitive, embarrassing, or they consider them irrelevant to the perceived survey objectives. Under the pressure of the survey interview, the interviewer may incorrectly skip over a question or fail to record an answer. Even when an answer is recorded on the questionnaire, it may be rejected during editing prior to analysis because it is inconsistent with other answers. The extent of item nonresponse varies according to the nature of the item and the mode of data collection. Often simple demographic items have few nonresponses, but items on income and expenditures may experience item nonresponse rates of 10% or more; extremely sensitive or difficult questions may be subject to high item nonresponse rates.

One common procedure for handling item nonresponse is to confine each analysis to those cases with responses to the items involved in that analysis. When dealing with univariate analyses, total and item nonresponse rates may be simply combined with this procedure. Thus, formula 26 for the bias of using the respondent mean to estimate the population mean may be applied, with the modification that W_m is now defined as the number of eligible elements failing to provide an answer to the item—through either total or item nonresponse—divided by the total number of eligible elements. The concerns about bias from total nonresponse thus apply equally to item nonresponse.

Corresponding to the weighting adjustments for total nonresponse, various *imputation* methods have been devised to try to compensate for the bias of item nonresponse. These methods operate by assigning values for the missing responses, using the responses to other items on the questionnaire as auxiliary information to aid in this process. One method divides the sample into classes on the basis of the responses to other relevant items, and then assigns the respondent class mean for the item in question for all the item nonresponses in that class. This method compensates for differential item nonresponse rates across the classes, and, with regard to estimating the population mean, it is equivalent to the weighting adjustments for total nonresponse based on the same classes.

The disadvantage of the class mean method is that it distorts the distribution of the item, creating spikes at the class means where all the item nonresponses are placed and, as a consequence, attenuating the variance of the distribution. A variant of this method that avoids this distortion is to assign for each item nonresponse one of the item responses in the same class. One version of this method, used by the U.S. Bureau of the Census, is sometimes known as the "traditional hot deck method." The classes are determined, and a single value of the item is assigned to each class, perhaps based on a previous survey. Then the current survey records are taken sequentially. If a record has a response for the item, its value replaces the value stored for its class. If the record has a missing response, it is assigned the value currently stored in its class. This method has a major attraction of computing economy because all the imputations are made from a single pass through the data file. It suffers the disadvantage, however, that a single response may be donated to several nonresponses; this will occur when within a class a record with a missing value is followed by one or more other records with missing values. Another version of this method minimizes the multiple use of responses by first sorting all the records into classes and then matching responses and nonresponses; this version also avoids the need to specify start-up values. It is the basis of a sophisticated imputation method used by the Bureau of the Census for the March Income Supplement of the Current Population Survey (Welniak and Coder, 1980).

Another type of imputation method employs a regression equation to predict the missing values, using the responses to other items on the questionnaire as predictor variables and determining the regression coefficients from the respondent sample. The imputed values can be taken as the predicted values from the regression, but when this is done the variance of the item distribution will be attenuated, as with the class mean method. A modification of this procedure to avoid this attenuation generates the imputed values by adding random residuals to the regression predictions.

A major benefit of imputation is that a data set with no missing values is constructed, a feature that greatly facilitates survey analyses. It is, however, important for the survey analyst to be aware of the fact that imputation has been used. Imputed values should be flagged in the data set so that the analyst can distinguish between real and imputed values. A survey data set containing imputed values should not be analyzed uncritically as if all the data were real values. One reason is that this procedure will attribute greater precision to the survey estimates than is justified. A second reason is that while imputation is likely to reduce the biasing effects of item nonresponse on univariate analyses, it can distort the associations between variables and hence have damaging effects on multivariate analyses. See Kalton and Kasprzyk (1982) for a review of imputation procedures and their effects on survey estimators.

10. SURVEY ANALYSIS

The analysis of survey data can employ any of a wide range of statistical techniques, many of which are discussed in other papers in this series. This section does not attempt to review these techniques, but instead discusses only the special considerations involved in analyzing data obtained from a complex sample design. The two topics treated here are the use of weights in survey analysis and the calculation of sampling errors for estimates based on complex sample designs.

Weights

Weights are used to assign greater relative importance to some sampled elements than to others in the survey analysis. Weights are needed when the sampled elements are selected by unequal probability sampling; they are also used in poststratification and in making adjustments for total nonresponse. We start with an illustration of the use of weights in the analysis of a nonepsem design, and afterward discuss other applications.

To illustrate the application of weighting procedures with a manageable example, we will consider a small sample size of ten. Suppose that the only list available for selecting a sample of students in a college is the combination of the class registers for each of the courses. An equal probability sample of listings is taken from this list—say by systematic sampling—with the associated student then being included in the sample. Let the total number of listings be 970, with a 1 in 97 sample of them yielding the sample of ten listings. Since the majority of students take more than one course and since they differ in the numbers of courses they take, the epsem sample of listings produces a nonepsem sample of students. The greater the number of courses a student takes, the greater is the student's selection probability.

Suppose that one objective of the survey is to estimate the mean number of textbooks purchased, with the numbers of textbooks purchased by the ten students and the numbers of courses they are taking being given in Table 5. The simple mean number of textbooks purchased is $\Sigma y_i/n = 47/10 = 4.70$. This is clearly a biased estimate of the mean number of books purchased by all the students in the college because of the unequal selection probabilities and the association between the selection probabilities and textbooks purchased. Inspection of the data in Table 5 shows that the more courses attended, the more textbooks the student is likely to buy, so that the simple sample mean will tend to overestimate the population mean. To compensate for the nonepsem design, weights that are inversely proportional to the selection probabilities are needed. If an element's selection probability is p_i, the weight should be k/p_i, where k is any constant chosen for convenience.

One obvious choice for k is k = 1, so that the weight $w_i = 1/p_i$. Thus, with the listings being sampled at a rate of 1 in 97, the weights for the sampled students would be $97/r_i$, where r_i is the number of courses taken by the ith student. Student 1 would have a weight of 97, student 2 a weight of 48.5, student 3 a weight of 32.3, and so on. The choice of k = 1 can be useful when estimates of population totals are required, such as the total number of textbooks purchased by the college's students, for with k = 1 the population total is simply estimated by the weighted sample sum $\Sigma w_i y_i$. However, often the selection probabilities are small and awkward numbers to handle, in which case an alternative choice of k may be used to simplify the weights. If a value other than k = 1 is used, the weighted sample sum $\Sigma w_i y_i$ has to be divided by k to estimate the population total; however, no adjustments are needed for means, percentages, variances, and other statistics that are averaged over the sampled values.

A second obvious choice of weights is to make them equal to the reciprocals of the numbers of courses taken, $1/r_i$, since it is the variable number of courses that gives rise to the unequal selection probabilities. These weights would then be 1.00 for the first student, 0.50 for the second, 0.33 for the third, and so on. This scheme, which implicitly employs a value of k = 1/97, is entirely acceptable, but it requires some rounding for 1/3. To avoid this rounding, the weights adopted in Table

5 are set equal to $12/r_i$ (implicitly choosing $k = 12/97$). When weights are used the sample mean is defined as

$$\bar{y}_w = \Sigma w_i y_i / \Sigma w_i$$

Here $\bar{y}_w = 217/54 = 4.02$, a value appreciably smaller than the seriously biased simple mean $\bar{y} = 4.70$.

Since $w = \Sigma w_i$ in the denominator of $\bar{y}_w$ is not fixed but would vary from sample to sample, the weighted mean is a ratio mean. As discussed in Chapter 6, the ratio mean is a biased estimator of the population mean, but the bias is negligible providing the coefficient of variation of the denominator is less than 0.1. Treating the sample of listings as an SRS and ignoring the fpc term, the variance of the weights may be estimated by

$$v(w) = n s_w^2 = n\Sigma(w_i - \bar{w})^2/(n - 1) = 624/9 = 69.33$$

Thus the estimated coefficient of variation of w is given by

$$cv(w) = \frac{se(w)}{w} = \frac{\sqrt{v(w)}}{w} = \frac{8.327}{54} = 0.15$$

Although in excess of 0.1, this coefficient of variation is small enough to ensure that the bias of the ratio mean is not appreciable. Since the coefficient declines with increasing sample size, it would clearly not be a matter of concern with a realistic larger sample size.

The estimated variance of the weighted mean is also that of a ratio mean, as discussed in Chapter 6. For the application of the theory of the ratio estimator, $\bar{y}_w$ may be written as $\Sigma u_i/\Sigma w_i = u/w$, where the variable u_i is defined as $u_i = w_i y_i$. Then, providing the coefficient of variation of w is less than 0.2, an approximate variance estimator for $\bar{y}_w$ is given by

$$v(\bar{y}_w) = [v(u) + \bar{y}_w^2 v(w) - 2\bar{y}_w c(u,w)]/w^2$$

which is simply equation 23 in the current notation. Using the data in Table 5, the following calculations may be made:

$$v(u) = n\Sigma(u_i - \bar{u})^2/(n - 1) = 3241/9 = 360.11$$

$$c(u,w) = n\Sigma(u_i - \bar{u})(w_i - \bar{w})/(n - 1) = 52/9 = 5.78$$

TABLE 5
Number of Textbooks Purchased and Number of Courses
Being Taken by the Ten Sampled Students (hypothetical data)

Student Number	Number of Textbooks (y_i)	Number of Courses (r_i)	Weight $w_i = 12/r_i$	$u_i = w_i y_i$
1	2	1	12	24
2	5	2	6	30
3	6	3	4	24
4	8	3	4	32
5	3	2	6	18
6	7	4	3	21
7	6	4	3	18
8	3	2	6	18
9	5	3	4	20
10	2	2	6	12
	47		54	217

Hence

$$v(\bar{y}_w) = \left[\frac{3241}{9} + \left(\frac{217}{54}\right)^2 \frac{624}{9} - 2\left(\frac{217}{54}\right)\left(\frac{52}{9}\right) \right] / 54^2 = 0.4915$$

and $se(\bar{y}_w) = 0.70$.

It is useful to compare the precision of this nonepsem sample with that of an SRS of the same size. For this purpose an estimate of the element variance of the numbers of textbooks purchased is needed. An estimate of this quantity is provided by

$$s_w^2 = \frac{n}{n-1} \frac{\Sigma w_i (y_i - \bar{y}_w)^2}{\Sigma w_i} = 4.382 \qquad [27]$$

Thus, for an SRS of 10 the variance of the sample mean is estimated, ignoring the fpc, by $v(\bar{y}_0) = s_w^2 / 10 = 0.4382$. The estimated design effect for the nonepsem sample is then

$$d^2(\bar{y}_w) = v(\bar{y}_w)/v(\bar{y}_0) = 0.4915/0.4382 = 1.12$$

indicating an increase of variance of about 12% as a result of the unequal selection probabilities. A loss of precision is usual when unequal selection probabilities occur as a result of frame deficiencies, and the loss can be substantial when the selection probabilities vary a great deal. For this reason, substantial variability in selection probabilities should be avoided whenever possible in this type of situation.

As a second example of the need for weights in dealing with a sampling frame deficiency, consider the frame problem of listings of clusters of elements. Suppose that an epsem sample of $\underline{a}$ dwellings is selected from the A dwellings in a city, and that one adult is sampled at random from each selected dwelling using the Kish selection grid. The probability that adult β in dwelling α is selected for the sample is given by the selection equation

$$P(\alpha\beta) = P(\alpha)P(\beta|\alpha) = (a/A)(1/B_\alpha)$$

where B_α is the number of adults in dwelling α. To compensate for the adults' unequal selection probabilities, weights proportional to $1/P(\alpha\beta)$ = AB_α/a are needed in the analysis. One obvious simple choice of weighting scheme for this case is to assign a weight to each sampled adult equal to the number of adults in his or her dwelling (i.e., B_α). (Although these weights are theoretically needed, in practice they are often not used because they vary little, the variation in number of adults per dwelling being slight. Thus they generally have only a negligible effect on the survey estimates [see Kish, 1965: 400]).

Another example of a sample design that gives rise to unequal selection probabilities is disproportionate stratification. Chapter 4 described how an estimate of the population mean can be computed by first calculating the sample means in each stratum and then combining these estimates into a weighted average $\bar{y}_{st} = \Sigma W_h \bar{y}_h$. An alternative procedure is to assign weights to each sampled element, with the same weight for all elements in one stratum, but different weights between strata, and then to use $\bar{y}_w$. The weights are made proportional to the inverses of the selection probabilities in each stratum; i.e., $w_{hi} = kN_h/n_h$ for all sampled elements in stratum h. It then follows that

$$\bar{y}_w = \underset{h\ i}{\Sigma\Sigma} w_{hi} y_{hi} / \underset{h\ i}{\Sigma\Sigma} w_{hi} = \underset{h}{\Sigma} kN_h \bar{y}_h / \underset{h}{\Sigma} kN_h = \underset{h}{\Sigma} W_h \bar{y}_h$$

so that $\bar{y}_w$ and $\bar{y}_{st}$ are equivalent. In this case $\bar{y}_w$ is not a ratio mean since its denominator is a fixed constant. The use of $\bar{y}_w$ rather than $\bar{y}_{st}$ has an advantage of computational convenience: Once weights have been assigned, standard computer programs for weighted data can be applied to obtain the survey estimates.

Weighting may also be applied in a similar way with the technique of *stratification after selection,* or *poststratification.* With this technique, knowledge of the population distribution of some supplementary variable (or variables) is used in the analysis to improve the precision of the sample estimators. Thus, for instance, if the age distribution of the population is known from a recent census, the sample can be divided into age groups, the means of survey variable y can be calculated for each age group ($\bar{y}_h$), and these means can be combined into the overall estimate $\bar{y}_{ps} = \Sigma W_h \bar{y}_h$, where W_h is the proportion of the population in age group h. As with disproportionate stratification, the poststratified mean can be alternatively expressed as a weighted mean, where each element is assigned a weight proportional to N_h/n_h. Ignoring for the moment issues of nonresponse and noncoverage, poststratification adjusts the sample distribution across the strata, which is subject to chance fluctuations, to make it conform to the known population distribution. Providing the expected sample sizes in the poststrata are ten or more, the variance of the poststratified mean is approximately equal to that of a proportionate stratified mean based on the same strata. Poststratification is useful in situations where the W_h are known but where the stratum to which each element belongs cannot be determined at the selection stage. Prior stratification cannot be used in such situations; however, information can be collected from sampled elements during the survey to enable them to be allocated to strata, thus allowing the use of poststratification. Poststratification can also be usefully employed to take advantage of additional stratification factors beyond those used at the design stage. As with proportionate stratification, gains in precision from poststratification accrue to the extent that there is heterogeneity between, or equivalently homogeneity within, the strata in terms of the survey variables.

Weighting of a sample to a known population distribution adjusts not only for sampling fluctuations but also for nonresponse and noncoverage (the failure of some elements to be included on the sampling frame). If, say, the nonresponse rate is higher among young people, or if more of them are missing from the sampling frame, weighting the sample to make if conform to a known age distribution compensates for these factors. It should be observed here, however, that the compensation is achieved by weighting up the respondents in the given age groups. To the extent that there are differences in the survey variables between the respondents and nonrespondents in each age group, some nonresponse bias will remain.

Like poststratification, the preceding weighting adjustment for nonresponse and noncoverage requires knowledge of the population distribution of some auxiliary variable, such as age, from an external source. Another type of nonresponse adjustment depends only on internal information in the sample, but that information has to be available for both respondents and nonrespondents. Information on the strata or PSUs in which the elements are located is often used for this type of adjustment. Suppose, for instance, that the sample is divided into geographical regions and, within regions, into classes according to whether the sampled element is situated in a rural, suburban, or central-city location. With an epsem sample, adjustments for variation in nonresponse rates across the resulting classes can be made by assigning weights of n_h / r_h to the respondents in class h, where n_h is the total sample size selected, and r_h is the achieved sample of respondents, in that class. These adjustments make the respondent sample distribution conform to the total sample distribution across the classes, again with the respondents in a class being weighted up to represent the nonrespondents in that class. This type of adjustment is addressed only at nonresponse—not at noncoverage.

In practice, the development of weights can become a complicated task, because a combination of adjustments is often required. In the first place, weights may be assigned to adjust for unequal selection probabilities, then these weights may be revised to adjust for differential response rates within classes of the sample, and finally further revisions may be made to adjust the sample distributions to known population distributions. Careful attention is needed to the development of weights, because serious errors are easily made.

Sampling Errors

As we have seen in the discussion of various sample designs, the extent of sampling error in survey estimators depends on the survey's sample design. The regular standard error formulae found in statistics texts and incorporated in most computer programs relate only to unrestricted sampling (simple random sampling with replacement). These formulae should not be applied uncritically with other sample designs, for which they may produce overestimates or, more often, underestimates of the sampling error.

In the case of simple random sampling without replacement, the variance of the sample mean is smaller than that of the mean from an unrestricted sample of the same size by the factor $(1 - f)$, the finite population correction term. When the population is large, the sampling fraction f is usually small, and the fpc term is approximately 1. In this situation the standard error formulae for unrestricted sampling may be applied satisfactorily with an SRS design.

A proportionate stratified design with SRS within strata gives estimators that are at least as precise as those produced by an SRS design; the estimators will be more precise to the extent that the strata are internally homogeneous with regard to the survey variable under consideration. The application of the standard error formulae for unrestricted sampling with this type of design will thus tend to overstate the sampling error in the survey estimates. When the fpc term can be neglected and when the gains in precision from stratification are small, the use of the unrestricted sampling standard error formulae may serve adequately. Before placing reliance on these formulae it is, however, advisable to carry out some checks to determine whether it is reasonable to ignore the gains from stratification.

The situation with disproportionate stratified sampling is more complex in two respects. In the first place, since disproportionate stratification is a nonepsem design, the application of the unrestricted sampling standard error formulae requires the use of weighted estimates of the population parameters involved. For instance, the standard error of a sample mean from an unrestricted sample is $\sigma/\sqrt{n}$; if this formula were applied with a nonepsem design, the population element variance σ^2 should be estimated by the weighted s_w^2 given in equation 27. Second, the effect of disproportionate stratification on the precision of the survey estimates is not clear-cut as in the case of proportionate stratification: Disproportionate stratified sampling may yield estimators that are more precise or less precise than those obtained from an unrestricted sample of the same size, depending on the allocation of the sample across the strata. Assuming survey element costs are the same for all strata, optimum (Neyman) allocation of the sample for estimating the population mean of a particular variable will produce a sample mean at least as precise as one based on a proportionate allocation, and more precise when the element variance of the variable varies across strata. The unrestricted sampling standard error formula will therefore tend to overestimate the sampling error of this mean. The use of the unrestricted sampling standard error formulae may, however, tend to underestimate the sampling errors of other estimates from this design.

Often disproportionate stratification is used to provide separate estimates for various domains of study, with the strata representing the smaller domains being sampled at higher rates in order to give adequate domain sample sizes. This use of disproportionate allocation often leads to a loss of precision in the overall estimates, and the loss can be severe when some domains are sampled at much higher rates. As a simple illustration, consider two strata, each of which is a domain of study for which separate estimates are required, with one stratum containing 90% and the other 10% of the population, and suppose for simplicity that the two strata have the same means and variances. If samples of the same size are selected from each stratum, weights in the ratio of 9:1 are required for the two strata in forming overall estimates. Ignoring the fpc term, the effects of these weights is to increase the variance of the overall sample mean by a factor of 1.64 compared with an unrestricted sample of the same size. When a marked variation in weights is needed to adjust for unequal selection probabilities, a substantial loss in precision can result. In consequence, the use of the unrestricted sampling standard error formulae can seriously underestimate the sampling errors of the survey estimates.

Clustering leads to a loss of precision compared with an SRS of the same size whenever the cluster intraclass correlation coefficient ρ is positive, as is almost always the case. The loss depends both on the magnitude of ρ and on the average subsample size selected per cluster, as discussed in Chapter 5. When the average subsample size is large, the loss can be serious even when ρ is relatively small. The unrestricted sampling standard error formulae thus tend to underestimate, often to a substantial extent, the sampling errors of estimates based on multistage clustered samples.

In practice, sample designs are often complex, involving both multi-stage sampling and some form of stratification at each of the sampling stages. Frequently proportionate stratification and epsem, or approxi-mately epsem, designs are used. The common empirical finding from sampling error computations that have been performed for estimates based on such designs is that the losses of precision from clustering tend to outweigh the gains from proportionate stratification, so that the complex sample design provides less precise estimators than an unre-stricted sample of the same size; that is, the design effects are greater than 1. The magnitude of the design effect depends on a multitude of factors, including the nature of the clusters, the average subsample size per cluster, the stratification used, the variable or variables under study and the form of the estimator. Thus, for instance, in national area probabil-ity samples, design effects for means and proportions of basic demo-graphic variables such as age and sex are generally near 1, reflecting the fact that geographical clusters exhibit little internal homogeneity in these variables. Design effects for socioeconomic and related variables, however, are generally greater than 1 because of the tendency of people in the same socioeconomic group to live in the same neighborhoods. Design effects for means or proportions of a subclass of the population that is fairly evenly spread across the clusters—termed a "crossclass"—are as a rule less than those for the equivalent means or proportions based on the total sample. Design effects for the differences between two subclass means are usually lower than the design effects for the subclass means themselves. Design effects for regression coefficients are often similar to those for differences between means. Whatever the estimators, however, design effects with complex sample designs are nearly always greater than 1, sometimes only slightly but sometimes substantially. The use of the unrestricted sampling standard error formulae thus generally overstates the precision of survey results based on such designs.

In recent years a number of computer programs have been developed to calculate sampling errors of estimates based on complex sample designs; see Kaplan and Francis (1979) for a list of some such programs. Mostly these programs treat the primary sampling units (PSUs) as being sampled with replacement, although in practice sampling without replacement is generally used. Treating the PSUs as if they had been sampled with replacement leads to an overestimate of variance, but the amount of overestimation is slight providing the first-stage sampling fraction is small. The major advantages of the with-replacement assumption are computing economy and generality. As shown in Chapter 5, if the first-stage sampling fraction is small, the standard error of the sample mean may be simply estimated from the variation between PSU totals; no estimates need to be made of the sampling variation within the PSUs, a feature that creates a substantial computational saving. More important, however, is the generality that goes with the assumption: Under the with-replacement assumption a single standard error formula for a particular estimator applies, no matter what form of subsampling is used within the PSUs. Thus, for instance, the same formula applies whether the elements are sampled (1) by SRS within the selected PSUs, (2) by systematic or stratified sampling, or (3) with further sampling stages and stratification. This generality is appealing not only because a single program will produce the standard error of a given estimator for any form of subsample design but also because the user of the program is not required to supply the program with details about the subsample design. The use of these programs requires only that each survey data record contains a code to indicate to which PSU it belongs, together with provision of information about the first-stage stratification.

Several general approaches exist for estimating sampling errors of estimators based on complex sample designs. One of these is the *Taylor expansion* or *delta method,* which has already been referred to in the discussion of the ratio mean in Chapter 6 (see formula 23). The basic procedure is to obtain a linear approximation for the estimator, and then to use the variance estimator for the linear approximation to estimate the variance of the estimator itself. The approach is most easily applied, and most widely used, for simple estimators. Many of the programs for computing variances of sample means, proportions, subclass means and proportions, and differences between means and between proportions from complex sample designs use this method. As noted in Chapter 6, the appropriate use of the Taylor expansion method for estimating the variance of a ratio mean or proportion requires that the coefficient of variation of the denominator of the ratio is less than 0.2. Most programs provide the values of this coefficient in their printouts; especially in the case of subclass analyses, these values should be routinely reviewed to check that they are sufficiently small.

An alternative approach to standard error estimation is to design the sample to permit standard error estimates to be computed simply for any survey estimate. As described in Chapter 7, the method of replicated sampling achieves this objective by constructing the total sample as a combination of a set of independent replicates, each of an identical sample design. The variation between the individual replicate estimates then provides the basis of a simple standard error estimate for the combined sample estimate, no matter what the complexity of that estimate or of the replicate sample design. As already discussed, the serious drawback to the use of simple replicated sampling with multistage designs is the conflict between the need for sufficient replicates to provide standard error estimates of adequate precision and the desire to use a good deal of stratification to produce precise survey estimates; as a consequence of this conflict, simple replicated sampling is seldom adopted. In its place, techniques of pseudoreplication have been developed to take advantage of the simple replicated standard error estimator while providing as precise estimates of standard errors as possible and avoiding the restriction on stratification. We will briefly describe the method of *balanced repeated replications* (BRR), which is sometimes known as half-sample replication (Kish and Frankel, 1970, 1974; Frankel, 1971; McCarthy, 1966).

The method of balanced repeated replications is generally employed with a paired selection design in which exactly two PSUs are sampled from each stratum. As has been noted earlier, in many multistage designs PSUs are stratified to the point of selecting one PSU per stratum, in which case the collapsed strata technique is needed for variance estimation purposes; collapsing pairs of strata approximates the actual design by a paired selection design. With BRR, the two PSUs selected in each stratum are treated as having been sampled independently. Viewed from the perspective of replicated sampling, the sample can be considered as made up of two replicates, one comprising one of the two PSUs—selected at random—from each stratum and the other comprising the remaining PSUs. If z' denotes the sample estimate of the parameter Z (e.g., a regression coefficient) based on the first replicate, or half-sample, and z'' the corresponding estimate based on the second half sample, or complement, then from replicated sampling theory a variance estimate for $\bar{z} = (z' + z'')/2$ is given from equation 24 with $c = 2$ by

$$v(\bar{z}) = [(z' - \bar{z})^2 + (z'' - \bar{z})^2]/2 \qquad [28]$$

In practice, the overall estimate used for Z is $\tilde{z}$, obtained by pooling the two half-samples, but $\bar{z}$ and $\tilde{z}$ are usually extremely close. Hence, as an approximation, $\bar{z}$ may be replaced by $\tilde{z}$ in the above variance estimator.

The limitation of the simple replicated sampling variance estimator is that, being based on only one degree of freedom, it is too unstable to be of any real practical utility. The solution to this problem used in BRR is to repeat the process of forming half-samples from the parent sample, to compute variance estimates each time, and then to calculate the average of the variance estimates obtained. Thus, if z_t' denotes the sample estimate of Z based on the tth half-sample and z_t'' that based on its complement, a variance estimator for $\tilde{z}$ is given by

$$v(\tilde{z}) = \Sigma[(z_t' - \tilde{z})^2 + (z_t'' - \tilde{z})^2]/2T$$

averaging over T half-samples and their complements, and replacing $\bar{z}$ in equation 28 by $\tilde{z}$.

The above reasoning explains the "repeated replications" part of BRR. The "balanced" part relates to the manner in which the half-samples are chosen. The T half-samples are not chosen independently, but rather are chosen in a balanced way that produces an efficient overall variance estimator. In order to employ full balance, the number of half-samples T selected has to be greater than or equal to the number of strata and also a multiple of four. Thus, for instance, with 22 strata (i.e., 44 PSUs in the paired selection design), $T = 24$ half-samples are needed for full balance; with 47 strata, $T = 48$ half-samples are needed. If the calculation of z_t involves a good deal of computation, and if the number of strata is great, the computations needed for all the half-samples required for full balance may be excessive; in this case, various techniques are available to achieve partial balance with a smaller set of half-samples.

Jackknife repeated replications (JRR) is another variance estimation technique for use with complex sample designs (Frankel, 1971; Kish and Frankel, 1974). Like BRR, it employs a repeated-replications approach. With the JRR method, a replicate is constructed by dropping out a single PSU and weighting up the other PSUs in its stratum to retain the sample distribution across the strata. This operation is repeated a number of times, dropping a different PSU on each occasion. When the total number of sampled PSUs, $\underline{a}$, is small, each one of them may be dropped out in turn to create a replicates, but this completeness is not essential. All that is required is that at least one PSU is dropped from each stratum; if this is not done for one or more strata, the variance contribution of those strata will not be represented in the overall variance estimate. Letting z_{ht} denote the estimate of Z based on the tth replicate formed from stratum h, a JRR variance estimator for $\tilde{z}$ is given by

$$v(\tilde{z}) = \sum_{h=1}^{H} \sum_{t=1}^{t_h} (a_h - 1) (z_{ht} - \tilde{z})^2 / t_h$$

where a_h is the number of sampled PSUs in stratum h, and t_h is the number of replicates formed by dropping PSUs from stratum h. When each of the PSUs in the sample is dropped in turn, $t_h = a_h$. As this formula shows, an advantage of JRR over BRR is that it can readily handle designs other than the paired selection design (for which $a_h = 2$).

All the preceding variance estimation methods involve approximations, but simulation studies have shown that they all give reasonable results. The choice between them is largely to be made in terms of computing economy, availability of programs, and applicability for the required estimates and for the sample design employed. The Taylor expansion method is often preferred for relatively simple estimates, and BRR and JRR have the advantage of being readily applied for estimates of any complexity. The BRR method is mainly restricted to the paired-selection design, but this design fits most samples in practice. Where it does not, JRR may be preferred.

Surveys usually collect data on an extensive set of variables and produce numerous results on the variables and their relationships. Even with the availability of sampling error programs, it is seldom possible to compute standard errors for all the estimates in a survey report; even if it were possible to compute them, the report would become unwieldly if they were all included. For these reasons, survey analysts usually compute only the standard errors of major results, together with a selection of other standard errors. These computations are then used to develop generalized models from which other standard errors can be inferred (see, for instance, Kish, 1965: 574-582).

Further details on the practical estimation of survey sampling errors and the use of generalized sampling error models are provided in a review paper by Kalton (1977). The paper by Kish and Frankel (1974) discusses sampling error estimation methods with survey samples and presents results from a simulation study comparing the Taylor expansion, BRR and JRR methods.

11. SAMPLE SIZE

One of the first questions that arises in sample design is, "What sample size is needed?" The discussion of this question has been left until now because it depends on several aspects of the preceding material.

To describe the basic ideas, consider a simple example of a face-to-face interview survey that is to be conducted to estimate the percentage of a city's population of 15,000 adults who say they would make use of a new library if one were built. To determine an appropriate sample size, it is first necessary to specify the degree of precision required for the estimator. This is no easy task, and initially the degree of precision required is often overstated. Suppose, for instance, the initial specification calls for an estimator that is within 2% of the population percentage with 95% probability; in other words, the 95% confidence interval should be the sample percentage plus or minus 2%. This specification thus requires that 1.96 SE(p) = 2%, where p is the sample percentage. Assuming initially the use of simple random sampling, and ignoring the fpc term, $SE(p) \doteq \sqrt{PQ/n'}$, where P is the population percentage, $Q = 100 - P$, and n' is the initial estimate of the sample size. Thus $1.96\sqrt{PQ/n'} = 2$ or $n' = 1.96^2 PQ/2^2$. In order to determine n', a value is needed for P. Since PQ is largest at P = Q = 50%, a conservative choice is to set P equal to a percentage as close to 50% as is likely to occur. Suppose that P is thought to lie between 15% and 35%; then the conservative choice is P = 35%. With this choice, n' = 2185. If this initial sample size were small compared with the population size, so that the fpc term could be ignored, it would be the required sample size. In the present case, however, the fpc term should not be neglected. A revised estimate of the sample size to take account of the fpc term is obtained, with N = 15,000, as

$$n = Nn'/(N + n') = 1907$$

The above calculation assumes simple random sampling, and a modification is needed for other sample designs. The modification consists of multiplying the SRS sample size by the design effect for the survey estimator under the complex design. If a list of the city's adults were available in the above example, then an unclustered proportionate stratified sample might well be used. In this case, a somewhat smaller sample might suffice because of the gains in precision arising from the stratification. As has been noted earlier, however, the gains from proportionate stratification are generally small when estimating a percentage, so the reduction in sample size will often be modest. Say, in the present case, that the design effect for the sample percentage with a proportionate stratified design is predicted to be 0.97. Then the required sample size for an unclustered proportionate stratified design to give a confidence interval of within $\pm 2\%$ is $0.97 \times 1907 = 1850$.

If no list of the city's adults or dwellings is available, area sampling may be needed, perhaps first sampling city blocks, then listing dwellings within blocks, sampling dwellings in selected blocks, and finally sampling one (or more) adults from each selected dwelling. Stratification and PPS selection would almost certainly be used in such a design. Suppose that with a stratified multistage design in which an average of ten adults are to be sampled from each PSU (block), the design effect is predicted to be about 1.3. Then the required sample for this design would be $1.3 \times 1907 = 2479$.

Another factor that needs to be included in the calculation of sample size is nonresponse. Suppose that the response rate is predicted to be 75%. Then the selected sample size needed to generate the achieved sample of 2479 adults with the multistage design has to be set at $2479/0.75 = 3305$. Of course, this adjustment serves only to produce the desired sample size; it does not address the problem of nonresponse bias.

Having reached this point, the researcher may decide to review the initial specification of precision to see if it can be relaxed. Suppose that, on reflection, a confidence interval of $\pm 3\%$ is deemed acceptable. Then the selected sample size can be substantially reduced to 1581. In practice, the level of precision required for an estimator is seldom cast in concrete. In consequence, the sample size is usually determined from a rough-and-ready assessment of survey costs relative to the level of precision that will result. It should be noted that the selected sample size depends on predictions of a number of quantities, such as the percentage of the population who say they would use the library, the design effect, and the nonresponse rate. Errors in predicting these quantities cause the survey estimator to have a level of precision different from that specified, but that is the only adverse effect; the estimator remains a reasonable estimator of the population parameter.

Having fixed the required sample size, the next step is to determine the sampling fraction to be used. If the sample is to be drawn from the list of the city's 15,000 adults, consideration will need to be given to the possibility of blanks (deaths and movers out of the area) and foreign elements on the list as well as to the consequences of any linking procedure that might be employed in dealing with missing elements. If, say, 4% of the listings are blanks and no linking is employed, the sampling fraction will need to be set at $2479/(0.96 \times 15,000) = 0.172$, or 1 in 5.81, to yield a sample of 2479. In practice, this sampling fraction may then be rounded for convenience, perhaps to 1 in 5.8 or even 1 in 6, to yield expected samples of 2483 or 2400, respectively.

In the case of the multistage area sample, the sample design calls for a sample of dwellings, with one adult sampled per dwelling. Suppose that at a recent census the city contained 6500 occupied dwellings. This figure should first be updated to correct for changes that have occurred since the census date, and also adjusted for any differences between the survey and census definitions of the city boundaries. Suppose that, as a result of these adjustments, the current number of occupied dwellings in the city is estimated to be 6750. In addition to these adjustments, allowance also needs to be made for the fact that the survey's sampling operations will probably fail to attain as complete a coverage of the city's dwellings as the census enumeration; the coverage rate for the sample might, say, be estimated as 95% of that of the census. Using this coverage rate, a sampling fraction of $2479/(0.95 \times 6750) = 0.3866$, or 1 in 2.59 dwellings, is needed to give the desired sample of 2479 adults. As before, the sampling rate may be rounded for convenience to 1 in 2.6, accepting a marginally smaller expected sample size (2466) for the use of a simpler rate.

While the above example has served to bring out a number of the issues involved in choice of sample size, it is nevertheless an oversimplified representation. In practice surveys are multipurpose, with a substantial number of estimators needing to be considered. Moreover, these estimators are required not only for the total sample but also for a wide range of subclasses, perhaps for different regions of the country, for people in different age groups or different educational levels, and so on. A major reason for the large samples typical of many surveys is the need to provide adequate precision for subclass estimators and for differences between subclass estimators. Larger samples permit finer divisions of the sample for subclass analysis, and, in general, the larger the sample the more detailed the analysis that can be conducted. The choice of sample size often depends on an assessment of the costs of increasing the sample compared with the possible benefits of more detailed analyses.

12. TWO EXAMPLES

This section describes two sample designs in order to illustrate how the preceding techniques can be combined in practical applications. One example is a sample design for a national face-to-face interview survey in the United States and the other is a sample design for a telephone interview survey.

A National Face-to-Face Interview Survey

Both the Survey Research Center (SRC) at the University of Michigan and the National Opinion Research Center (NORC) at the University of Chicago maintain national probability sample designs for their face-to-face interview surveys of individuals, families, households and sometimes other units of inquiry. These sample designs are revised every decade to take advantage of up-to-date data provided by the decennial Census of Population and Housing. After the 1980 census, the two organizations collaborated to select their master samples according to a common sample design. The following paragraphs describe this design, which is a stratified multistage area sample using selection with probabilities proportional to estimated size (PPES) at the various stages.

The primary sampling units (PSUs) for the NORC/SRC national sample design are Standard Metropolitan Statistical Areas (SMSAs), counties, or groups of counties with a minimum 1980 census population of 4000 persons. The sixteen largest SMSAs (e.g., New York, Chicago, San Francisco, Boston, St. Louis, and Atlanta) are included in the sample with certainty. They are "self-representing PSUs," which are properly treated as strata. According to the following procedure, a sample of 68 PSUs was selected from the remaining PSUs by PPES sampling, where the size measure is the PSU's number of occupied housing units in the 1980 census. First, the PSUs were separated into 68 strata of approximately equal sizes (i.e., containing approximately equal numbers of housing units). These strata were formed by first dividing the PSUs into the four census regions (North Central, Northeast, South, and West) and within regions into SMSAs and non-SMSAs. The SMSAs were further stratified by geographical location and by the sizes of their largest cities. The non-SMSAs were further stratified by geographical location and by their overall sizes. One PSU was then selected with PPS from each of the 68 strata, with further control being applied to the pattern of selections across strata to ensure a good representation of PSUs in terms of other control variables, such as percentage Black in the rural deep South and percentage Hispanic in the West. (For a description of the technique of controlled selection, see Goodman and Kish, 1950; Hess et al., 1975.)

The next operation in the sampling procedure was the selection of smaller clusters within the 16 self-representing SMSAs and 68 sampled PSUs. The clusters chosen for this purpose were blocks in urban areas for which the census provides block statistics and enumeration districts elsewhere. A minimum size of 48 housing units was set for these clusters; where sizes fell below this minimum, geographically adjacent clusters were combined. These clusters comprise the second-stage units within the sampled PSUs, with six of them being selected from each sampled PSU for the main samples of each survey organization (SRC and NORC). Within the self-representing SMSAs, these clusters are in fact the PSUs. Six clusters were selected for each organization in each of the eight smallest self-representing SMSAs, but the large self-representing SMSAs warranted a greater number of sampled clusters. For instance, 24 clusters were selected in the New York SMSA and 18 clusters in the Los Angeles SMSA for the main samples of each organization.

The selection of clusters within the self-representing SMSAs and sampled PSUs was carried out by PPES sampling, again with the 1980 numbers of occupied housing units as the measures of size. Systematic sampling from an ordered list of clusters was used to give the gains of implicit stratification for the variables employed in the ordering. Within a self-representing SMSA or sampled PSU the clusters were ordered by county, by minor civil division (in some cases), by census tract or enumeration district number and by block number. Counties were ordered according to size and geography. In the twenty states for which information was available on the size and median family income of minor civil divisions (local government units such as cities and towns), the divisions were ordered by size and median income. Blocks and enumeration districts were sorted by census tract number and then by block or enumeration district number to generate a geographical ordering.

The sampled clusters resulting from this process varied markedly in size from 50 occupied housing units up to 700 or more. A further stage of sampling was employed in the larger clusters to reduce them to a more manageable size. This stage first required these clusters to be partitioned into clearly defined segments, with approximate measures of size being assigned to each segment. This operation was based on a scouting of the clusters by SRC and NORC field staff, in which they made a field count of the distribution of occupied housing units. Then one segment was selected from each large cluster with PPES.

The final stage of the sample design involved a listing by the field staff of the housing units in all the selected segments. These listings are then available for use as the frame for the selection of samples for a number of surveys. The method of sampling from the listings may well differ between surveys, and it may also differ between large and small segments. It is, of course, important to address the problem that the listings become out of date as time passes.

For other descriptions of national area sample designs, the reader is referred to U.S. Bureau of the Census (1978) for a description of the sample for the Current Population Survey, and to Kish (1965: chaps. 9 and 10).

A Telephone Interview Survey

The use of telephone interviewing for social surveys of the general U.S. population has increased substantially in recent years, at least in part in response to the existing high penetration of telephones. With about 93% of households having telephones in their housing units, telephone numbers provide an attractive sampling frame for many surveys. In considering a telephone survey, it should nevertheless be recognized that some 7% of households are not covered, and that these households are more heavily concentrated among low-income households, households in which the head is nonwhite and under 35, and households located in the South (Thornberry and Massey, 1978). In cases in which the survey's objectives require good representation of these subgroups, a telephone sample may need to be augmented by another sample—perhaps an area sample—in a dual frame design (see, for instance, Groves and Lepkowski, 1982).

Given that a survey of the general population is to be conducted by telephone, the question arises of what sampling frame to use for telephone households. One obvious choice is the published telephone directories, but they prove to be inadequate because so many telephone numbers are not listed. Over 20% of residential numbers are not included in the directories, because (1) they are recent movers, (2) the subscribers have paid to be unlisted, or (3) a clerical error was made in the preparation of the directory. Recognizing the potential bias resulting from these missing elements, various modifications have been suggested to sampling telephone numbers from directories, such as taking the sampled telephone number and adding a constant to the last digit or taking the number and substituting a random number for the last two digits (see Frankel and Frankel, 1977). Such methods do not, however, give each household a known and nonzero probability of selection, as required for probability sampling; consequently, they may produce biased estimates.

An alternative sampling frame is to take the set of all possible telephone numbers. In the United States telephone numbers are composed of ten digits in three parts, such as 301-555-1212, where the first part is the area code, the second part is the central office code, and the last four digits are the suffix. There are just over 100 area codes and over 30,000 central office codes (i.e., combinations of area and central office codes) in operation. Within a central office code 10,000 suffixes are available for use, but the majority of them are nonworking numbers and nonresidential numbers for businesses, pay telephones, and the like.

One way of sampling residential telephone numbers from this sampling frame would be to select an area code/central office code combination at random from a list of such combinations (an up-to-date list of these combinations is available from the Long Lines Department of American Telephone and Telegraph [AT&T]), and then to select a four-digit random number from 0000 to 9999 to constitute the suffix for the telephone number. This simple version of a random–digit dialing (RDD) procedure gives complete coverage of all residential numbers, but it suffers from the problem of many blanks (nonworking numbers) and foreign elements (nonresidential numbers) on the sampling frame. These blanks and foreign elements can of course simply be rejected, with the remaining sample constituting a valid probability sample of the residential numbers, but the procedure is costly because of the calls needed to eliminate the nonresidential numbers: On average about five telephone numbers need to be sampled to produce each residential number.

An alternative RDD scheme designed to reduce the number of unproductive calls is described by Waksberg (1978). This scheme views the frame of telephone numbers as a set of banks of 100 numbers each, the banks being defined by the area code/central office code combination and the first two digits of the suffix. Thus, within each area code/central office code combination, there are 100 banks of 100 numbers, that is, suffixes 0000-0099, 0100-0199, 0200-0299, . . ., 9900-9999. These banks are then used as PSUs in a two-stage design. The banks are sampled with equal probability, and one number is selected at random within the bank. If that number is not a residential number, the bank is rejected. If it is a residential number, an interview is attempted and additional random numbers are selected within the bank until a specified number of households is drawn.

With the Waksberg scheme, the probability that the αth bank is selected and accepted is proportional to the proportion of residential numbers it contains, $B_\alpha/100$, where B_α is the number of residential numbers in the bank. The probability of a specified residential number being selected given that bank α is accepted is $(b + 1)/B_\alpha$, where b is the number of additional residential numbers taken if the first number is a residential number. Thus the selection equation for residential number β in bank α is

$$P(\alpha\beta) \propto \frac{B_\alpha}{100} \cdot \frac{b + 1}{B_\alpha} = \frac{b + 1}{100}$$

Thus the scheme is an epsem one if exactly b additional residential numbers are selected per bank. In effect, the banks are PSUs sampled with exact PPS, size being the number of residential numbers in the PSU, and a fixed number of residential numbers is then taken in each selected PSU.

As we have seen, the use of two-stage sampling generally leads to less precise survey estimates than would a single-stage sample of the same size; that is, the design effect is almost always greater than 1. Two-stage sampling is then justified only when the economies associated with its use enable a sufficient increase in sample size to outweigh this loss of precision. The justification for the use of the Waksberg scheme comes from the greater proportion of residential numbers that it produces. With this scheme about two out of three numbers selected within the sample clusters are residential numbers, as compared with only one in five overall with the simple scheme described earlier.

The opportunities for stratification with telephone sampling are limited by the lack of information on good stratification factors. The frame of area code/central office code combinations available from AT&T provides information only on the vertical and horizontal coordinates of each exchange—a geographical unit covering either a group of central office codes or a single central office code—and the number of central office codes each exchange contains. From this information the sample can be stratified geographically (using exchange geographical coordinates) and by the size of exchange (using the number of central office codes covered by an exchange as an index of its size). Groves and Kahn (1979) provided further details and described the use of this information for implicit stratification, ordering the list of area code/central office code combinations by the stratification factors and then taking a systematic sample from the ordered list.

Some telephone surveys collect data on households, in which case the interviewer has to conduct the interview with a designated respondent or any one of a set of such respondents. Other surveys, however, collect data for specified individuals, often any adult, in which case the residential telephone number identifies a cluster of elements. This frame problem is often handled by selecting one eligible individual at random, with an appropriate weighting adjustment in the analysis. One way to proceed is to use the Kish selection grid as described in Chapter 8, but some researchers believe that the listing of eligible individuals along with their sexes and relative ages at the start of the interview (as the technique requires) is difficult for interviewers to handle and may give rise to a high refusal rate. Consequently, Troldahl and Carter (1964) have developed a technique that avoids the listing and requires interviewers to collect data only on the number of eligible individuals and the number of eligible males (or females) in the household. The interviewer then refers to a table with the number of eligible individuals along one axis and the number of eligible males along the other, and reads off the designated respondent from the appropriate cell; the cell may, for instance, specify that the "oldest man" is to be selected. As with the Kish selection grid, there are several versions of the table with different specifications of who is to be selected, and the tables are varied across the sample. With the Troldahl-Carter technique there are four tables, each of which is used with equal frequency. Bryant (1975) has suggested a modification of the technique to compensate for a shortage of men in the sample; her modification halves the use of one of the tables that selects a higher proportion of women. Although not unbiased, these alternative procedures are widely used in practice. (See Czaja et al., 1982, for a recent experimental comparison.)

Telephone surveys also face the frame problem of duplicate listings, for a small proportion of households have more than one telephone line. This problem can be handled by collecting information from each sampled household in the survey on its number of telephone numbers, and then incorporating a factor inversely proportional to this number in the weight for the sampled household or individual.

13. NONPROBABILITY SAMPLING

Although this paper has focused predominantly on probability sampling, the widespread use of nonprobability sampling methods makes it inappropriate to avoid mention of them entirely. This section discusses various types of nonprobability sampling, including the widely used technique of quota sampling.

The major strength of probability sampling is that the probability selection mechanism permits the development of statistical theory to examine the properties of sample estimators. Thus estimators with little or no bias can be used, and estimates of the precision of sample estimates can be made. The weakness of all nonprobability methods is that no such theoretical development is possible; as a consequence, nonprobability samples can be assessed only by subjective evaluation. Moreover, even though experience may have shown that a nonprobability method has worked well in the past, this provides no guarantee that it will continue to do so. Nevertheless, despite its theoretical weakness, various forms of nonprobability sampling are widely used in practice, mainly for reasons of cost and convenience.

One type of nonprobability sampling is variously termed *haphazard, convenience,* or *accidental sampling.* Here are some examples:

—volunteer subjects for studies;
—the patients of a given doctor;
—the children in a particular school;
—interviews conducted on a street corner;
—the respondents to a pull-out questionnaire included in a magazine;
—persons calling in response to a television request for opinions.

In view of the considerable risk of bias with such samples, it is dangerous to attempt to use their results to make inferences about general populations.

A second type of nonprobability sampling is known as *judgment* or *purposive sampling,* or *expert choice.* In this case the sample is chosen by an expert in the subject matter to be "representative," for instance, when an educational researcher chooses a selection of schools in a city to give a cross section of school types. In practice, different experts would rarely agree on what constitutes a "representative" sample, and in any case a judgment sample is subject to a risk of bias of unknown magnitude.

The concern about the bias of survey estimators from a judgment sample—or any nonprobability sample—increases with sample size. Consider the comparison of a sample estimator from a judgment sample and that from a probability sample of the same size. If the sample size is very small, the variance of the probability sample estimator will be large, so that in relative terms the bias of the judgment sample estimator may be unimportant. However, as the sample size increases the variance of the probability sample estimator decreases, while the bias of the judgment sample estimator may change little. This reasoning provides a justification for nonprobability samples when the sample size is small, with a change to probability sampling for larger sample sizes. Thus, for instance, if a researcher can conduct a study in only one or two cities, it is probably better to select the cities by expert choice rather than to rely on the vagaries of random chance, which could easily result in an odd sample. If, however, the sample size is increased to 50 cities, then a carefully stratified probability sample would almost certainly be preferable.

A third type of nonprobability sampling is known as *quota sampling.* This technique, of which there are many variants, is widely used by market researchers on the grounds that it is less costly, is easier to administer, and can be executed more quickly than a comparable probability sample. The essence of the technique is that interviewers are given quotas of different types of people with whom they are to conduct interviews. For instance, one interviewer may be assigned quotas of six men under 35 years old, five men 35 and older, five employed women, and eight unemployed women. The aim of assigning quotas of interviews in these four groups is to avoid, or at least control, the selection biases that would occur if the interviewers were given a free hand in their choice of respondents. The quota controls may be interrelated, as in the example just given, or they may be independent—for instance, specifying quotas of ten men and thirteen women, eleven persons under 35 and twelve persons 35 and older.

The early stages of sampling for a national quota sample are often carried out by probability methods in exactly the same way as for a national probability sample. The two types of sample then part company only at the final stage of selecting individuals for interview. With a probability sample, interviewers are required to interview specified persons selected by a probability mechanism, while with a quota sample they have only to complete their quotas, often with additional controls on the times of day at which they make their calls and on the routes they follow. Quota sample interviewers may, for instance, be instructed to seek eligible respondents for their unfilled quotas by working around sampled blocks in a defined way from specified starting points, interviewing no more than one respondent per dwelling.

In passing, it is worth commenting on the use of the control in quota sampling of no more than one respondent per dwelling. While this control spreads the sample across different dwellings and avoids the fieldwork problems associated with multiple interviews in a dwelling, it leads to an underrepresentation of individuals from large dwellings (Stephenson, 1979). Probability samples also, of course, often select only one person from each sampled dwelling; in their case, however, the use of weights inversely proportional to the selection probabilities in the analysis serves to correct for this underrepresentation.

The quota groups created by the controls in quota sampling are often likened to strata, since both represent population groups from which distinct samples are taken. Although the resemblance is instructive, it should not mask the major difference between the two types of grouping, namely that within strata, elements are selected by probability methods, and within quota groups they are not. This difference leads to different criteria for forming strata and quota groups. Since probability sampling avoids the risks of selection biases, the choice of strata needs to be concerned only with increasing the precision of survey estimators; as seen earlier, gains in precision are achieved by forming strata that are internally homogeneous in the survey variables. On the other hand, with quota sampling the dominant concern is to form groups in a way that minimizes selection biases. Forming quota groups that are internally homogeneous in the survey variables can be helpful for this purpose, but the chief consideration is to form groups that are internally homogeneous in the availability of their members for interview or, alternatively expressed, to form groups that differ from one another in their members' availability. This latter consideration led the National Opinion Research Center at the University of Chicago to employ the four quota groups cited earlier for the surveys based on "probability sampling with quotas" that it conducted in the 1960s and 1970s, namely: men under 35 (or under 30); men 35 and older (or 30 and older);

employed women; and unemployed women (Sudman, 1966; Stephenson, 1979). These controls were particularly designed to yield appropriate representation of the hard-to-find population groups of young men and unemployed women. A tight geographical control on interviewers' routes within sampled blocks with probability sampling with quotas was deemed sufficient to provide the samples with satisfactory racial and economic compositions.

Having chosen the quota groups, the interviewers' quotas are set by reference to data available on the population distribution across the groups, often derived from the decennial census. The quotas may be made more or less the same for all interviewers, being set according to the overall distribution of the survey population across the groups, or they may be varied to match the specific distributions in the sample areas in which the interviewers are working. To the extent that the data from which the quotas are determined are inaccurate (perhaps because they are out of date), the distribution of the quota sample will not conform to the true population distribution across the groups. This situation may be contrasted with a probability design that is self-correcting for such inaccuracies.

It is sometimes argued that quota sampling avoids the problem of nonresponse. In effect, however, what a quota sample does is to substitute an alternative respondent for an unavailable or unwilling respondent. As a consequence, although a quota sample produces the required distribution across the quota controls, it underrepresents persons who are difficult to contact or who are reluctant to participate in the survey. It is in fact more likely to underrepresent such persons than is a probability sample since, with the latter, interviewers are required to make strenuous efforts to secure interviews with the designated sample members.

Two main features explain the widespread use of quota sampling, despite its theoretical weaknesses. One is the lack of the need for a sampling frame for selecting respondents within sampled areas. The other is the avoidance of the requirement that interviewers make callbacks to contact specified respondents. With a quota sample, if an eligible person is unavailable when the interviewer calls, the interviewer simply proceeds to the next dwelling. Both features give simplicity and enable a survey to be carried out much more quickly with quota than with probability sampling. An associated factor is the lower cost of a quota sample. The cost of a quota sample, however, depends on the extent of the controls imposed: the less restrictive the controls, the lower the cost but, on the other hand, the greater the risk of serious selection biases.

14. CONCLUDING REMARKS

Survey sampling is a highly specialized and developed component of the survey process. There is a wide range of techniques available, and numerous pitfalls to avoid. The sampling novice needs to proceed with great caution, since it is all too easy for the utility of survey results to be seriously marred by mistakes made in sample design. For this reason, when embarking on a survey, the wisest course for a researcher with limited sampling knowledge is to consult an experienced practicing survey statistician.

There is a substantial body of both theoretical and practical literature on survey sampling. For reasons of space this paper presents only a broad overview of the subject, with the limited aim of enabling the reader to understand and appreciate the uses of the range of available techniques. Those readers requiring a more detailed treatment of the subject are referred to one of the specialist texts. Those by Kish (1965), Hansen et al. (1953), and Yates (1981) are particularly recommended for their discussions of sampling practice, and those by Cochran (1977), Sukhatme and Sukhatme (1970) and Murthy (1967) for their treatments of sampling theory. The notation and terminology used here have been made mostly consistent with that in Kish (1965) in order to facilitate cross-reference with that text. The book by Deming (1960), which advocates the wide use of replicated sampling, contains much good practical advice. At a less advanced level, the books by Raj (1972), Levy and Lemeshow (1980) and Sudman (1976) are useful. Stuart (1976) has illustrated the basic ideas of sampling nonmathematically with a small numerical example, and the chapters on sampling in Moser and Kalton (1971) provide an introduction to the subject.

REFERENCES

BLALOCK, H. M. (1972) Social Statistics. New York: McGraw-Hill.
BRYANT, B. E. (1975) "Respondent selection in a time of changing household composition." Journal of Marketing Research 12: 129-135.
COCHRAN, W. G. (1977) Sampling Techniques. New York: John Wiley.
CZAJA, R., J. BLAIR, and J. P. SEBESTIK (1982) "Respondent selection in a telephone survey: a comparison of three techniques." Journal of Marketing Research 19: 381-385.
DEMING, W. E. (1960) Sample Design in Business Research. New York: John Wiley.
DILLMAN, D. A. (1978) Mail and Telephone Surveys. New York: John Wiley.

FRANKEL, M. R. (1971) Inference from Survey Samples. Ann Arbor, MI: Institute for Social Research.

——— and L. R. FRANKEL (1977) "Some recent developments in sample survey design." Journal of Marketing Research 14: 280-293.

GOODMAN, R. and L. KISH (1950) "Controlled selection—a technique in probability sampling." Journal of the American Statistical Association 45: 350-372.

GROVES, R. M. and R. L. KAHN (1979) Surveys by Telephone. New York: Academic.

GROVES, R. M. and J. M. LEPKOWSKI (1982) "Alternative dual frame mixed mode survey designs." Proceedings of the Section on Survey Research Methods, American Statistical Association: 154-159.

HANSEN, M. H., W. N. HURWITZ, and W. G. MADOW (1953) Sample Survey Methods and Theory, Vols. 1 and 2. New York: John Wiley.

HESS, I., D. C. RIEDEL, and T. B. FITZPATRICK (1975) Probability Sampling of Hospitals and Patients. Ann Arbor, MI: Health Administration Press.

IVERSEN, G. R. and H. NORPOTH (1976) Analysis of Variance. Sage University Paper series on Quantitative Applications in the Social Sciences 07-001. Beverly Hills, CA: Sage.

KALTON, G. (1977) "Practical methods for estimating survey sampling errors." Bulletin of the International Statistical Institute: 47, 3: 495-514.

——— and D. KASPRZYK (1982) "Imputing for missing survey responses." Proceedings of the Section on Survey Research Methods, American Statistical Association: 22-31.

KAPLAN, B. and I. FRANCIS (1979) "A comparison of methods and programs for computing variances of estimators from complex sample surveys." Proceedings of the Section on Survey Research Methods, American Statistical Association: 97-100.

KENDALL, M. G. and B. B. SMITH (1939) Tables of Random Sampling Numbers. Cambridge: Cambridge University Press.

KISH, L. (1965) Survey Sampling. New York: John Wiley.

———(1962) "Studies of interviewer variance for attitudinal variables." Journal of the American Statistical Association 57: 92-115.

——— and M. R. FRANKEL (1974) "Inference from complex samples." Journal of the Royal Statistical Society B 36: 1-37.

———(1970) "Balanced repeated replications for standard errors." Journal of the American Statistical Association 65: 1071-1094.

LEVY, P. S. and S. LEMESHOW (1980) Sampling for Health Professionals. Belmont, CA: Lifetime Learning Publications.

McCARTHY, P. J. (1966) Replication. An Approach to the Analysis of Data from Complex Surveys. Vital and Health Statistics Series 2, No. 14. Washington, DC: Government Printing Office.

MOSER, C. A. and G. KALTON (1971) Survey Methods in Social Investigation. London: Heinemann.

MURTHY, M. N. (1967) Sampling Theory and Methods. Calcutta: Statistical Publishing Society.

O'MUIRCHEARTAIGH, C. and S. T. WONG (1981) "The impact of sampling theory on survey practice: a review." Bulletin of the International Statistical Institute 49(1): 465-493.

RAJ, D. (1972) The Design of Sample Surveys. New York: McGraw-Hill.

STEEH, C. G. (1981) "Trends in nonresponse rates, 1952-1979." Public Opinion Quarterly 45: 40-57.

STEPHENSON, C. B. (1979) "Probability sampling with quotas: an experiment." Public Opinion Quarterly 43: 477-495.

STUART, A. (1976) Basic Ideas of Scientific Sampling. London: Griffin.

SUDMAN, S. (1976) Applied Sampling. New York: Academic.

——— (1966) "Probability sampling with quotas." Journal of the American Statistical Association 61: 749-771.

SUKHATME, P. V. and B. V. SUKHATME (1970) Sampling Theory of Surveys with Applications. London: Asia Publishing House.

THORNBERRY, O. T. and J. T. MASSEY (1978) "Correcting for undercoverage bias in random digit dialed national health surveys." Proceedings of the Section on Survey Research Methods, American Statistical Association: 224-229.

TROLDAHL, V. C. and R. E. CARTER (1964) "Random selection of respondents within households in phone surveys." Journal of Marketing Research 1: 71-76.

U.S. Bureau of the Census (1978) The Current Population Survey: Design and Methodology. Technical Paper 40. Washington, DC: Government Printing Office.

WAKSBERG, J. (1978) "Sampling methods for random digit dialing." Journal of the American Statistical Association 73: 40-46.

WARWICK, D. P. and C. A. LININGER (1975) The Sample Survey: Theory and Practice. New York: McGraw-Hill.

WELNIAK, E. J. and J. F. CODER (1980) "A measure of the bias in the March CPS earnings imputation system." Proceedings of the Section on Survey Research Methods, American Statistical Association: 421-425.

YATES, F. (1981) Sampling Methods for Censuses and Surveys. New York: Macmillan.

GRAHAM KALTON is a research scientist in the Sampling Section of the Survey Research Center and professor of biostatistics at the University of Michigan. His previous appointment was professor of social statistics at the University of Southampton in England, and before that he was reader in social statistics at the London School of Economics. He has published articles on survey sampling and survey methodology, and his books include An Introduction to Statistical Ideas for Social Scientists *(1966),* Survey Methods in Social Investigation, *coauthored with Sir Claus Moser (second edition, 1971), and* Compensating for Missing Survey Data *(1983).*